Computer Appreciation

T. F. FRY A.C.W.A., A.M.B.I.M., F.I.D.P.

Senior Lecturer in Computer Studies
Cassio College, Watford, Herts.

LONDON
BUTTERWORTHS
1970

ENGLAND: BUTTERWORTH & CO. (PUBLISHERS) LTD.
LONDON: 88 Kingsway, W.C.2

AUSTRALIA: BUTTERWORTH & CO. (AUSTRALIA) LTD.
SYDNEY: 20 Loftus Street
MELBOURNE: 343 Little Collins Street
BRISBANE: 240 Queen Street

CANADA: BUTTERWORTH & CO. (CANADA) LTD.
TORONTO: 14 Curity Avenue, 374

NEW ZEALAND: BUTTERWORTH & CO. (NEW ZEALAND) LTD.
WELLINGTON: 49/51 Ballance Street
AUCKLAND: 35 High Street

SOUTH AFRICA: BUTTERWORTH & CO. (SOUTH AFRICA) LTD.
DURBAN: 33/35 Beach Grove

Standard Book Number: 406 72700 7

Printed in Great Britain at
the St Ann's Press, Park Road, Altrincham

Preface

The rapidly growing demand for basic Computer Studies in Colleges and Schools, and the increasing number of examinations in this subject introduced by national examining bodies, has led to the preparation of this book. The three main factors I have tried to keep in mind while writing it are: firstly, the syllabuses of examining boards, in particular the requirements of the Royal Society of Arts (Computer Appreciation examinations), the Institute of Data Processing (Certificate and Diploma examinations), and the computer content of the Ordinary National Diploma and Ordinary National Certificate in Business Studies. With the aim of helping students and teachers of Computer Appreciation and Computer Technology, I have included at the end of each chapter a selection of typical examination questions suitable for written work or for classroom discussion; secondly, I have tried to keep the style as simple and as non-technical as possible so that students reading for interest only will not find the going too laborious; thirdly, I have tried to keep in mind the organisation that is thinking of changing over to computer processing and needs some idea of what it is all about and what management problems are likely to arise.

I am aware, in as new a subject as this, of the many problems involved in both teaching and writing about it. In particular, in the field of 'hardware', to describe in detail the capabilities of all the machines available would be impractical in a book of this nature. Computer experts will, I feel, forgive me if I have been guilty at times of over-simplification. In trying to cover basic ideas on such a wide range of subject matter it is most probable that some points have been missed. I will be most grateful to readers for suggestions for any additional aspects of the subject that could well have been included.

Finally may I express my thanks to the Royal Society of Arts and to the Institute of Data Processing for permission to reproduce their past examination questions, to International Computers Ltd. for many of the illustrations in this book and to Mr. J. Parfitt, Tutor Librarian of Cassio College, Watford, for his invaluable help in reading the text and compiling the index.

T. F. FRY

Contents

Figures

1

The Development of Computers

Few technological developments of recent times have had as wide-spread an effect on industry, commerce and the public generally as the development of the Electronic Computer. It has been suggested that the advent of the computer heralds a second Industrial Revolution. The introduction of industrial machinery can be likened to an extension of man's hands, the computer represents an extension to his mind. Electronic computers have certainly outstripped the human mind in the speed with which they can absorb information, process it and communicate the results, the reliability with which they can carry out repetitive operations and their capacity to store vast quantities of information and to retrieve any item in a very short time.

With the advance of technology and the increase in commercial activity over the centuries, man has long been concerned to fashion tools to help him control these activities and to compile the records arising from them. The electronic computer is the latest and most sophisticated tool devised for this purpose, but it is more easily understood when seen as a development of previous devices. The following is an account of some of these tools that have been developed in the past.

DEVELOPMENT OF CALCULATING DEVICES

The Abacus

Some doubt exists about the origin of the Abacus although it is widely believed that its earliest use was in Egypt. It probably developed through the use of clay tablets into which grooves were cut side by side and allowed to harden. Pebbles were placed in, or taken away from these grooves, as numbers were added or subtracted. Later, holes were made through the pebbles and they were threaded on wires or strings and mounted in a frame. Values were given to the rows of pebbles or beads, unit values for the top row and increasing in multiples of ten downwards. In fig. 1.1 the beads in row A have unit values, those in row B each have a value of 10, those in row C, 100 and so on. To represent the number 248, eight beads in row A are moved to the right, four in row B and two in row C. To add 354 to this number, first the units are added, 8 and 4. The two beads remaining on the left of row A are moved to the right, then all ten moved back to the left and the ten carried down by moving one bead in row B to the right, the remaining two units are now moved to the right in row A. Alternatively, a quicker way, since 8 plus 4 equals 12, is to move six beads in row A from right to left leaving two on the right, and move one additional bead in row B to the right. Next, for the tens, move five beads in row B to the right. This means that all the beads in this row are now on the right and so can be moved back and one bead in row C moved to the right to carry down the 100. Finally a further three beads in row C are moved to the right.

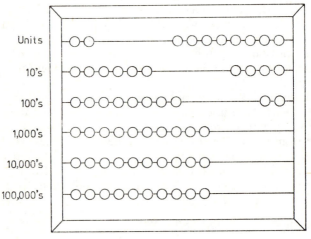

Fig. 1.1—The number 248 on an Abacus

In skilled hands the Abacus is a very fast and efficient method of dealing, not only with addition and subtraction, but also, using the principle of repetitive addition and subtraction, of multiplication and division.

Napier's Rods and Bones
As an astronomer, John Napier was continually involved in the need to make quite complex calculations and found it difficult to find people able to carry these out accurately. In 1614 he wrote

commenting on 'this tedious expense of time' and the 'many slippery errors' to which these calculations were subject. 'I began to consider in my mind by what certain and ready art I might remove these hindrances.'

Fig. 1.2—Napier's Rods

His considerations led to the development of a ready reckoner known as 'Napier's Rods.' It consists of nine pieces of card about an inch wide, each divided vertically into nine squares (see fig. 1.2). Each square is divided diagonally from the top right-hand corner to the bottom left-hand corner, and on each card is written a multiplication table, from 1 to 9, placing the tens above the diagonal and the units below. This gives a ready reckoner capable of multiplying two numbers. For example, to multiply 4,587 by 863, take the four cards representing the 4, 5, 8 and 7 tables and place them side by side in this order. Starting with the units, 3, add diagonally carrying one to the left when necessary. Then proceed in the same manner with the tens and the hundreds. The sum of the answers will give the product of 4,587 × 863 (see fig. 1.3).

One great disadvantage in using cards for this method of calculating is that each table is represented once only so that, using just the nine tables, it becomes impossible to work a problem in which the same digit occurs more than once. To overcome this Napier designed four-sided rods with a different table on each of the four sides of each rod. These rods were made from bone and became known as 'Napier's Bones.' In this way each table was represented four times increasing the adaptability of the method.

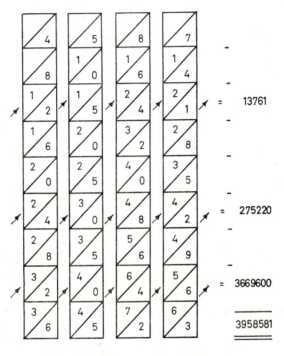

Fig. 1.3—4,587 × 863 using Napier's Rods

Pascal's Adding Machine

It was not long after Napier had developed his ready reckoner that the first mechanical aid to calculating was produced in the mid-seventeenth century. This was a machine in the sense we would use the word today with wheels, gears and dials. The son of a superintendent of taxes in Paris, Blaise Pascal wanted to produce a machine that would help his father. In 1642, at the age of 18, he produced a device that was probably the world's first adding machine. It consisted of a number of wheels each divided into ten segments and capable of being rotated through any number of these. The wheels were connected with each other by a 'carry-over' lever so that, on ten being registered on one wheel a carry over of one was made to the next. The position of the wheels at any time showed the total contents of the machine.

Pascal's device was, however, only an Adding Machine and there was a need for a machine to carry out more involved calculations including multiplication and division. It was not until some 50 years later that the first of these was developed.

Gottfried Wilhelm von Leibnitz

Working on the principle that multiplication can be treated as repetitive addition and division as repetitive subtraction, Leibnitz, when he was 25 years old, built a machine that would carry out the four basic arithmetic rules, addition, subtraction, multiplication and division. This machine was manufactured in 1694. The device made use of a drum on which nine teeth were mounted, one nine-tenths the length of the drum, the next eight-tenths and so on. This meant that at one end of the drum nine teeth were mounted round its circumference, decreasing by one at a time along the length of the drum until at the other end there were none. A shaft was mounted parallel to the length of the drum on which was mounted a gear wheel which could be moved into any position. On rotating the drum, the teeth engaged with the gear wheel moving this through the number of teeth corresponding to the number of teeth at this position on the drum. To multiply by 6, for instance, the gear wheel was moved opposite the 6 position on the drum. One revolution moved the gear wheel through six teeth, two revolutions through twelve and so on. By mounting a number of these drums side by side to represent multiples of 10 and incorporating suitable carry-over mechanisms, any number could be set up on the gear wheels and multiplied by the number of revolutions through which the drums were turned. By reversing the direction of the drums repetitive subtraction, or division, could be carried out.

Little further development seems to have been made in Adding or Calculating machines for the next 150 years. In 1820, Thomas de Colmar first produced commercial calculating machines, based on the Leibnitz 'Stepped Drum' principle. Between 1870 and 1880, in Sweden, Colonel Odhner produced a wheel device to replace Leibnitz's drum. On this wheel, by manipulation of a key board, a varying number of teeth can be set which engage in a normal gear wheel when revolved. This is the principle used in most rotary desk calculators to-day. In 1885 Alexander Burroughs developed and marketed in America an Adding Machine with a 'full' key-board, that is a key for every value in every position.

Charles P. Babbage

The next landmark in the development of calculating machines and indeed, what is considered to be the fore-runner of the modern computer, was brought about by an English mathematician, Charles P. Babbage, in the early nineteenth century. Charles Babbage was born in Devonshire in 1792 into a rich banking family. No great attention seems to have been paid to his formal education but his main interest appears to have been in mathematics which he taught himself to the extent that, when he went up to Cambridge he found his own knowledge of the subject already wider than that of his tutor. In 1828 he was awarded the Lucasian Chair of Mathematics, a post that he held for eleven years without delivering a single lecture at the University.

Unlike most great mathematicians of the day, he was not just concerned with theory, but was interested in the application of mathematics to everyday problems. His dissatisfaction with the accuracy of mathematical tables used by the Analytical Society (which he had earlier formed) led him to conceive the idea of developing a machine that would produce these tables automatically and accurately.

The principle upon which Babbage was to build his machine had not been used before and was based on the level difference between values computed for a formula. The following table shows the level difference between values or x^2 in the formula $y = x^2$

Value of x	Value of y	1st level diff.	2nd level diff.
0	0		
		1	
1	1		2
		3	
2	4		2
		5	
3	9		2
		7	
4	16		2
		9	
5	25		2
		11	
6	36		

Since the second level difference is constant, corresponding with the second power of x in $y=x^2$, y can be found for any value of x by simple addition. If, for example, $x=7$, then $y=2+11+36=49$. Further numbers in the first difference can be found by successive additions of 2, from which further values of y can be found. Because of the use of this principle, Babbage called his device a 'Difference Engine'.

He built a small working model that was exhibited in 1822. This was received with such great interest and enthusiasm that the Royal Society persuaded the Government to give financial support to the development of the idea. Babbage worked for several years on the project without producing the results hoped for by the Royal Society. This was due in part to the inability of industry to manufacture the parts required to the very narrow tolerances specified resulting in Babbage having to make them himself, but in greater part to the fact that the more he thought about the machine the more ambitious his ideas became. Finally he was planning a very complex device which he called an 'Analytical Engine' which included the principles of programming, a computer memory and an arithmetic unit.

In view of this, the Government, having contributed some £17,000 towards the development, then withdrew their support and future work had to be financed by Babbage himself. While no complete working model of his Analytical Engine was ever made, Babbage, when he died in 1871, left thousands of drawings showing how the machine could be built.

From this point onwards a number of people in different countries were concerned in the further development of computing aids.

Punched Cards

Punched Cards were originally developed as an aid to textile production by a Frenchman, Joseph M. Jacquard. Working in a silk-weaving factory in Lyons he saw that one of the main problems in weaving was the control of the large numbers of needles used to give a required pattern. He conceived the idea of using cards perforated with holes in such a way that only those needles required for a given pattern would be actuated. When a different pattern was required the card was changed. It is interesting to note that Charles Babbage planned to make use of this idea for presenting numbers to his Analytical Engine.

Punched Cards were first used for data processing by Dr. Hollerith in America who adapted the principle in order to record data from a national census conducted by the United States Government in

1890. Each position on the card was made to represent a pre-determined item of information and holes were punched in the relevant positions to record the information. Dr. Hollerith, with his assistant Powers, also developed machines for sorting and analysing the information recorded in the cards. Realising the potential of punched cards in classifying and recording commercial data led Hollerith and Powers to develop a range of machines for commercial use. This consisted of Punches for preparing cards, sorters for putting cards into any required sequence and Tabulators to print the information contained in the cards, these also incorporated adding registers for summarising quantitative data.

Broadly speaking, these machines were developed along two parallel channels, the Hollerith Company using cards with 80 recording columns and the Powers-Samas Company cards containing 40 columns. By various mergers the Hollerith Company eventually became part of International Business Machines (IBM), and the Powers-Samas Company, merging with the British offshoot of Hollerith, British Tabulating Machines (BTM) became International Computers and Tabulators (ICT) which by further mergers has today become International Computers Ltd. (ICL).

DEVELOPMENT OF COMPUTERS

It is probably correct to say that the first computer was built at Harvard University, U.S.A. and was put into service in 1944. This put into practice many of the concepts formulated by Charles Babbage 100 years or so earlier but made use of up-to-date electro-mechanical techniques which resulted in a far more sophisticated machine than that planned by Babbage. It was called an Automatic Sequence-controlled Calculator and could perform any sequence of operations involving addition, subtraction, multiplication, division, comparison of numbers and reference to stored tables. Different tables could be stored for the solution of specific problems. Input was by Punched Cards or Switches and output to Punched Cards or Electric Typewriter.

The first all-electronic computer was built at the University of Pennsylvania, to solve problems in ballistics and aeronautics for the U.S. Army. Taking some three years to construct it finished up as a massive machine weighing some thirty tons and using 18,000 electronic valves and diodes. It occupied some 1,500 square feet of floor space. Put into service in 1946 it was known as the ENIAC (Electronic Numerical Integrator and Calculator) but was relatively unadaptable as it had been designed to work on specific problems.

The next machine developed by the University of Pennsylvania, also for the U.S. Army and known as EDVAC (Electronic Discrete Variable Automatic Computer), was far more versatile. This was a stored program machine using a Punched Paper Tape input and has been described as the world's first commercial electronic data processing machine.

About the same time IBM were developing general purpose computers in the United States resulting in the introduction in 1948 of the IBM 604, and the IBM 701 in 1952. By 1960 the IBM 650 with Punched Paper Tape as well as Punched Card input and using Magnetic Tape was well established in use.

Parallel with this development in America, research and development was going on in Britain. At Cambridge University a team led by Dr. M. V. Wilkes were working on a machine known as EDSAC (Electronic Delay Storage Automatic Computer). The association of J. Lyons and Co. Ltd., with Dr. Wilkes' team led to the production of the first computer for commercial use in this country, the LEO, ('Lyons Electronic Office'). This became operational in 1951. Manchester University in the meantime had started work on MADAM (Manchester Automatic Digital Machine) the first of which, known commercially as the Ferranti Mark 1, was installed in 1953. During the late 1940's and early 1950's development was going on in a number of universities and commercial companies. Birkbeck College, London, produced the first computer using Magnetic Drum Storage, ARC (Automatic Relay Calculator) and later the 'All Purpose Electronic Computer' (APEC) was built for the British Tabulating Machine Company. From this was developed the HEC 1, shown in 1952 at the Business Efficiency Exhibition. English Electric Ltd., also working in the field, produced the ACE (Automatic Computing Engine) and from this developed, in 1955, a commercial data processing machine called DEUCE.

In the late 1950's the electronic valve was superseded by transistors and the first all-transistor computers built. At this stage several companies in the U.S.A., were involved in the manufacture of machines, Honeywell introducing their Honeywell General Purpose machine in 1960, the National Cash Register Company their National 304 in 1959 and the Radio Corporation of America their RCA 501 in the same year. Meanwhile, the first all-transistor Computer in Britain was built. In 1964 both IBM in America and ICT in Britain announced new ranges of computing systems, IBM their 360 series and ICL their 1900 series. Both series showed a new approach to the supply of Computers by providing a range of machines, all compatible within their series, with different capacities, powers and speeds, and with alternative input, output and storage devices.

IMPACT OF COMPUTERS

Earlier in this chapter it was said that the suggestion had been made that the advent of the computer heralds a second Industrial Revolution. Be this as it may, it is certainly true to say that the developing use of computers is having very far-reaching effects both in Commerce and Industry, and from a national and social point of view. The computer is a most powerful tool, and if used wisely, and in the right context can do much to alleviate the burden of repetitive donkey-work, increase efficiency in commerce and industry and speed new developments in technology. On the other hand, like any other tool, it can be abused to the detriment of the individual. It could make easier the imposing of stricter controls over, and the increasing of interference into, the lives of people and the promotion of changes in working conditions and environment for which people have not been fully prepared.

Social Effects

Perhaps, at any rate in their early stages of development, computers were endowed by the public with an air of mystery probably fostered by the use of such descriptions as 'Electronic Brains' and by an emphasis on their capacity to remember and make decisions. This gave rise to fears that computers would 'take over' both in the 'big brother' sense and by performing a great deal of semi-skilled work, make many workers redundant.

As far as the latter is concerned, while it is true that two important functions of computers are to process the mass of facts and figures arising in any commercial enterprise, and to increase automation by automatic control in production processes, experience has shown that fears of redundancy are to a large extent unfounded. With nearly 2,000 computers in operation in this country there seems to be little sign of large-scale redundancy arising from their use. The introduction of the computer, in itself, has opened up new areas of work both for their users and their manufacturers, and it is often possible for the user to absorb some of his staff whose work has been taken over, into the new computer department. However, to be realistic, there will be people in individual installations who cannot be so absorbed and who are faced with losing the work they may have been doing over a long period of time. In these circumstances companies should provide facilities for re-training, with the object of transferring the people concerned to other areas of work within the organisation. If necessary, they should also put a brake on the recruitment of new employees until all the people disturbed by the introduction of the computer have been re-settled.

As far as the former attitude is concerned, (the 'take-over' in the 'big brother' sense), perhaps this concern is not quite so unfounded. It is a fear in many peoples minds that as Central and Local Government Departments make increasing use of computers to store their Income Tax records, Health records, Car records, Census records and so on, a point may be reached at which our lives are too much of an open book to any person with access to the computer files. It would seem to be reasonable that safeguards should be provided to guard against the misuse of information stored centrally in computers.

Apart from the fears which may arise from the widespread use of computers, the practical effects of their introduction have been becoming more apparent over the past few years. Our Electricity and Gas accounts have taken on a new form. When we pay them we are instructed 'do not fold', otherwise the computer will be unable to digest them. Our signature, on its own, is no longer sufficient for our bank, we have to have account numbers as well. We are presented with documents printed in strange characters with which we are unfamiliar. These are some of the more noticeable effects of computers in our daily life and we must expect their influence to become more marked as their use extends.

Impact on Industry and Commerce

While the effects of the introduction of Computers on Industry and Commerce are discussed in more detail in the chapter on Management, the following observations are made at this point. It would be easy to say that the effect of computers is to raise commercial and industrial efficiency, reduce costs and to increase productivity. This, however, would be rather too sweeping a generalisation to make. Benefits do not accrue automatically simply by buying and installing a machine, they will depend to a great extent on the following factors:

(a) The attitude of top management.
(b) The attitude of departments making use of the services available from a computer department.
(c) The co-operation of staff at all levels in implementing the changes in organisation and procedures that are necessary.

(d) The degree of efficiency and control with which the computer
department operates.
(e) The reliability and timeliness of source data.
(f) The mechanical efficiency and suitability of the machines used.
(g) The acceptability of the computer output reports.

However, given the most vital condition, the full support of
management at the highest level, a skilled computer team working
with adequate machine resources should be able to achieve a level
of efficiency in processing information, in controlling commercial
and industrial activity and in exploiting new technological developments that will lead towards the optimum use of technical and
human resources.

EXERCISES CHAPTER 1.

1.   What benefits would you expect to result from the installation
of a computer in a Commercial organisation?
2.   'The computer is just a tool to save a lot of donkey-work in
offices'. Explain in what ways you feel this statement falls
short of the capabilities of a computer installation.
3.   Outline the conditions you think necessary for the efficient
working of a computer department.
4.   What do you think are the main differences in principle between
an electro-mechanical accounting machine and an electronic
computer?
5.   Give an account of the development of aids to calculating
up to the introduction of the modern computer.
6.   'Computers are a boon to mankind'. Discuss this statement
giving reasoned arguments and facts to support your con-
clusions.
              (Royal Society of Arts-Computer Appreciation Stage 1)
7.   Give an account of the part played by Charles P. Babbage
in the development of mechanical aids to calculating.

2

Basic Elements of a Computer

Before considering in detail how the various parts of a Computer work, let us try to get a picture in broad outlines of what a computer is and does. This can probably best be done by breaking down a simple office job into its component parts.

A clerk working in a stock control section has to price requisitions passed to him from a materials store. These requisitions contain the following information:

Description and Part-number of the articles issued from store.

Quantity issued.

Number of the job on which the articles are used.

Date, requisition serial number, and a signature.

On receipt of the requisition the clerk is required to enter in the relevant column the unit price of the article, which is obtained by reference to a price-list. He then multiplies the unit price by the quantity and enters the product in the £·p column. Should there be more than one line entry on the form he will have to add the column and enter the total at the bottom.

To complete this task, the Stock Control Clerk will have to perform a sequence of operations something like this: (see Figure 2.1)

(a) Read the information appearing on the requisition.

(b) Refer to a Price-list to obtain the unit price of the article.

(c) Multiply the unit price by the quantity.

(d) Enter the answer to (c) and total if necessary.

Taking a closer look at these operations we can identify them as follows:

(a) Read the information appearing on the requisition—here the clerk is accepting information for processing—we can call it the INPUT of the procedure

(b) Refer to a price-list to obtain the unit price—this is reference to stored or filed information—we can call it STORAGE

(c) Multiply the unit price by the quantity—this is the ARITH-METIC of the procedure

(d) Enter the answer to (c) in the £·p column—this is the OUTPUT.

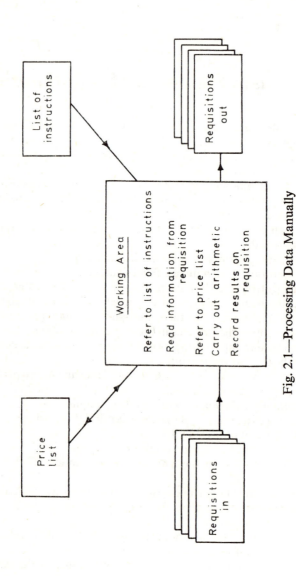

Fig. 2.1—Processing Data Manually

The procedure then has four distinct elements:

INPUT   STORAGE   ARITHMETIC   OUTPUT

but in order to get the correct answer, the operations must be carried out in a pre-determined sequence. We could make a more detailed list of instructions, in sequence, which could well take this form:

1. Read part-number from the requisition.
2. Look up part-number in price list, read price and enter it in the unit price column.
3. Read quantity from requisition.
4. Multiply quantity by unit price.
5. Write answer to (4) in £·p column.
6. If there is another entry on the requisition start again at (1) if not carry on at (7).
7. Add the £·p column.
8. Write total at bottom of column.
9. If there is another requisition go back to (1) if not stop.

Since the correct operation of this procedure depends upon the observation of this sequence of instructions, we should add a fifth to the four elements listed above. We can call this a PROGRAM. However, we must remember that the program is not part of the information to be processed but the list of instructions that have to be followed to give the correct answer. The name we usually give to the information for processing is DATA, and so the program is applied to the data in order to give the required results. We must also remember that the program has to be stored. If we are new to a job we may keep the program jotted down on a piece of paper to which we can refer as we go along. Later, as we become more experienced, we will probably memorise the program and carry out the instructions automatically. But whether on paper or in our head, the program is stored.

We start, then, with data recorded on a requisition form and at the end we have an answer recorded in £·p. In between them there is a 'working area' in which we refer to the program, refer to the data on the requisition and to the price list. We carry out a simple calculation and note the answer down on the original requisition.

There is still one further factor we must bear in mind. It would be most unusual to have a clerk working away on these requisitions without being supervised. Someone has to make sure that the instructions are being carried out correctly, that the requisitions are available when required, that the correct price-list is being used and so on. In other words, there must be an element of CONTROL over the whole proceedings.

Now a computer works very much like this:

The original information, recorded in one way or another, is read in to the machine	INPUT
The completed answer is read out of the machine	OUTPUT
And in between is the 'work area' which we call the	CENTRAL PROCESSOR
In which reference is made to the stored data and the stored program	STORAGE
And also in which the calculations are carried out	ARITHMETIC
And the whole proceedings supervised by	CONTROL

We will see later that the internal storage capacity of the Central Processor is not always sufficient to hold the program required and all of the data as well, so supplementary external stores are used to which reference can be made in a very short time.

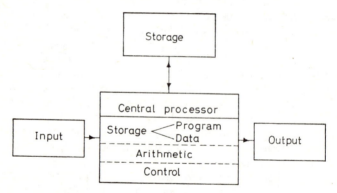

Fig. 2.2—Basic Elements of a Computer

Basically then, a complete computer configuration consists of a central device known as a Central Processor with a number of devices surrounding it that are used for specialised purposes. (See fig. 2.2). There are Input Devices for reading and transferring data and programs to the processor, Output Devices for accepting information from the processor and devices, usually known as Backing Stores, for storing additional data. These devices surrounding the central processor are called PERIPHERALS (See fig. 2.3).

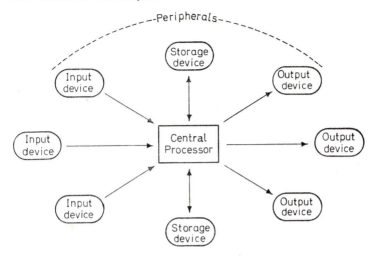

Fig. 2.3—Elements of a Computer Configuration

For a Computer Installation to operate we must have a Central Processor and the Peripherals to support it, which are commonly known as the HARDWARE of an installation. In addition we need the programs to direct the computer and the Systems on which it will work, collectively known as the SOFTWARE.

While these basic elements of a computer are dealt with in detail in later chapters, let us now take a brief look at each of them.

Central Processor

The main features of a central processor are its capacity to store and manipulate data. This storage capacity is sometimes known as the computer's memory. However, when all is said and done a computer in only a machine, and can only retain information presented to it in the simplest of forms. In fact the computer's memory is only required to remember sequences of two distinct characters (0 and 1) and all information presented to it is coded in this form. This is a numbering system known as Binary. Of course it would be a very laborious process if all numeric and alphabetic information had to be changed to this form by hand before it was fed to the machine, so the computer is designed to do this for itself. In the same way it will convert the results of its calculations from Binary form back to the numbers and letters we normally use. On the surface this may appear to be a very complex and costly method of working out what are comparatively simple problems. The advantage of a computer is in its high speed, which can process data many thousand times faster than manual methods.

Input

Unfortunately, it is usually not possible to feed data into a computer in the form that it originates. If we could feed the actual requisition mentioned earlier into the machine, get the machine to do the required 'working out' and write the answer in the correct place, then eject the completed requisition from the other end, things would be a lot more straightforward. However, there are difficulties that prevent a computer from doing this. For example, the requisitions may be of different shapes and sizes with writing in different positions. The form of handwriting may differ so much from requisition to requisition that we could well have difficulty in reading it ourselves let alone in expecting a machine to do so. To get over these problems the information must be:

(a)   prepared on a standard size and type of form that the machine will always be able to accept and

(b)   recorded in such a way that the machine will be able to recognise it and read it.

The usual way of doing this is to convert the information into holes punched in cards or in a continuous strip of paper tape giving each letter, number and symbol a distinctive pattern of holes that the computer will recognise. These two forms of input are known as Punched Cards and Punched Paper Tape, and are prepared on machines by an operator from the original data.

Output

While the information read into a computer will probably be in the form of punched holes and the central processor will deal with this in binary coded form, these two forms would nearly always be unacceptable as a method of communicating the results of the computer's work. It is the function of an output device to present these results in a readable and usable form. This is usually accomplished by using a printer which converts the coded computer results into conventional numbers, letters and symbols.

EXERCISES CHAPTER 2

1.   A computer consists of a central processor supported by a number of peripherals. What do you understand by the term

'peripheral'? Explain why these are necessary and give examples stating the purpose of each.

2. What do you understand as the basic elements of a computer? Using any illustration of your own choice, explain how these play their part in processing data.

3. Distinguish between the Hardware and the Software of a computer installation.

4. What is a computer program? Explain why a program is essential in working out a problem by computer.

5. What are the main functions of a Central Processor?

6. Compare a digital computer with a calculating machine and outline the advantages and disadvantages of the computer.

(Royal Society of Arts—Computer Appreciation Stage 1)

3

Binary Arithmetic

There are, in common use, a variety of numbering systems with which we are very familiar. For example, when measuring time we know that 60 seconds equal one minute, 60 minutes equal one hour and 24 hours equal one day. Again in linear measurements, twelve inches equal one foot, three feet equal one yard and so on. In money we know that two half-pennies equal one new penny and 100 new pennies equal £1.

In all of these systems a 'carry-over' occurs when a given number is reached:

45 secs+30 secs	=15 carry 1	=1 min 15 secs.
8 ins+9 ins	=5 carry 1	=1 foot 5 ins.
£0·63p+£0·72p	=35 carry 1	=£1·35p
$14\frac{1}{2}$p+$7\frac{1}{2}$p+$36\frac{1}{2}$p	=58 carry 1	=$58\frac{1}{2}$p.

The most commonly used of these is the Decimal or Denary system having a carry-over factor of 10. The value of each digit in a decimal expression is governed by its place in the expression. In the number 4,695 we know that the right-most digit is equal to 5 units, the next left equals 9 tens, the next 6 hundreds and the left-most digit 4 thousands. Each digit then, reading from right to left, represents a multiple of a successively higher power of 10, where $10^0=1$, $10^1=10$, 10^2 (ten squared)$=10 \times 10=100$ and so on.

$$4,695=(4 \times 10^3)+(6 \times 10^2)+(9 \times 10^1)+(5 \times 10^0)$$
$$= \ 4,000 \ + \ 600 \ + \ 90 \ + \ 5 \qquad =4,695$$

Use of a number system based on 10 involves the use of a collection of 10 symbols, 0, 1, 2, 3, 4, 5, 6, 7, 8, 9.

In a computer the use of such a wide range of characters is inconvenient, and use is made of a range containing only two characters, 0 and 1. This is known as the Binary system which, as a matter of fact we use every day when converting half-pence to new pence. That is $\frac{1}{2}$p+$\frac{1}{2}$p+$\frac{1}{2}$p=1 carry 1=$1\frac{1}{2}$p

In a Decimal system a carry-over occurs each time ten is reached and is indicated by moving a one to the left followed by a zero. In a Binary system a carry-over occurs each time two is reached and is indicated in the same way by moving a one to the left followed by a zero.

In Decimal 5+5=10 (Decimal ten)
In Binary   1+1=10 (Decimal equivalent two) and
                1+1+1=1 carry 1=11 (Decimal equivalent three)

In a Decimal system place values increase by an additional power of 10 moving from right to left of an expression, in a Binary system these place values increase by additional powers of 2.

Place values in a Decimal system 10^4, 10^3, 10^2, 10^1, 10^0.

Place values in a Binary system 2^4, 2^3, 2^2, 2^1, 2^0.

(remember, $2^0=1$, $2^1=2$, $2^2=4$, $2^3=8$ and so on)

This means that in the Binary expression 11101, we have, reading from left to right:

$$(1 \times 2^4) + (1 \times 2^3) + (1 \times 2^2) + (0 \times 2^1) + (1 \times 2^0)$$
$$= \quad 16 \; + \; 8 \; + \; 4 \; + \; 0 \; + \; 1 \quad = \text{Decimal 29.}$$

CONVERSIONS FROM ONE NOTATION TO THE OTHER

Decimal to Binary

The principle used here is to divide the Decimal number successively by two until it is reduced to zero. Each time, when on division by two there is a remainder of one this one becomes a Binary digit 1, and when the remainder is 0 this becomes a Binary 0. The Binary expression is built up from right to left.

Example: To convert Decimal number 343 to Binary.

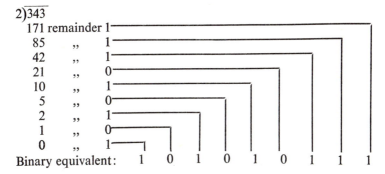

```
2)343
   171 remainder 1
    85    ,,     1
    42    ,,     1
    21    ,,     0
    10    ,,     1
     5    ,,     0
     2    ,,     1
     1    ,,     0
     0    ,,     1
Binary equivalent:   1   0   1   0   1   0   1   1   1
```

Binary to Decimal

The Decimal value of a Binary expression is equal to the sum of the Decimal values of the Binary digits.

Example: To convert Binary number 111011 to Decimal.

$$1 \quad 1 \quad 1 \quad 0 \quad 1 \quad 1$$
$$= 2^5 + 2^4 + 2^3 + 0 + 2^1 + 2^0$$
$$= 32 + 16 + 8 + 0 + 2 + 1 = \text{Decimal 59}$$

Binary Fractions

In a Binary integer, successive places to the left increase in value by an additional positive power of two. In a Binary fraction, successive places to the right decrease their value by an additional negative power of two.

Binary fraction $\cdot 1 \quad = 2^{-1} \qquad\qquad = \frac{1}{2} \quad = \cdot 5$ Decimal fraction

$\qquad\quad \cdot 01 \quad = 2^{-2} = \quad \dfrac{1}{2 \times 2} \quad = \frac{1}{4} \quad = \cdot 25$ „ „

$\qquad\quad \cdot 001 \quad = 2^{-3} = \quad \dfrac{1}{2 \times 2 \times 2} \quad = \frac{1}{8} \quad = \cdot 125$ „ „

$\qquad\quad \cdot 0001 = 2^{-4} = \dfrac{1}{2 \times 2 \times 2 \times 2} = \frac{1}{16} = \cdot 0625$ „ „

Conversion of Decimal to Binary fraction

Multiply the Decimal fraction successively by two, counting each 10 carry-over as a Binary 1, and if there is no carry-over count as a Binary 0. Discard the carry-over for the purpose of the next multiplication. The Binary expression is built up from left to right.

Example: To convert Decimal fraction $\cdot 625$ to a Binary fraction.

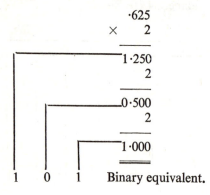

```
                    ·625
              ×        2
              ─────────────
           │ 1·250
           │          2
           │    ─────────────
           │    │ 0·500
           │    │        2
           │    │   ─────────────
           │    │   │ 1·000
           │    │   │ ═════════
    1    0    1    Binary equivalent.
```

Conversion of Binary fraction to Decimal fraction

The Decimal value of the Binary expression is equal to the sum of the Decimal values of the Binary places.

Example: To convert Binary fraction ·1101 to a Decimal fraction.

$$
\begin{array}{llll}
 & 1 & 1 & 0 & 1 \\
= & 2^{-1}+2^{-2}+0+2^{-4} \\
= & \tfrac{1}{2}\ +\tfrac{1}{4}\ +0+\tfrac{1}{16} \\
= & \cdot5\ +\cdot25+0+\cdot0625 \\
= & \qquad\quad \cdot8125\ \text{Decimal fraction.}
\end{array}
$$

CALCULATIONS IN BINARY

Addition

As, in the case of Decimal addition, one is carried to the left each time ten is reached, so in the case of Binary addition one is carried to the left each time two is reached. The simple rules are:

$$0+0=0$$
$$0+1=1$$
$$1+1=0 \text{ carry } 1$$
$$1+1+1=1 \text{ carry } 1$$

Example.

Decimal		*Binary*						
106		1	1	0	1	0	1	0
+124		1	1	1	1	1	0	0
carry 1		1	1	1	1			
230		1	1	1	0	0	1	1	0

Note a carry-over does not occur in this example until the fourth pair of Binary digits from the right. Here $1+1$ equals 0 carry 1 and the carry 1 is the digit shown below the line under the fifth pair of digits. Here $0+1+$carry 1 equals 0 carry 1, the carry 1 being shown below the line under the sixth pair of digits where $1+1+1$ equals 1 carry 1, this pattern repeating itself for the seventh pair.

Subtraction

In Decimal subtraction, when taking a larger number from a smaller number, one 'ten' is carried from the left and compensated for by adding one to the next left digit to be subtracted similarly in

Binary one 'two' is carried from the left and added back to the next left Binary digit to be subtracted.

The simple rules are:

    0−0=0
    1−0=1
    1−1=0
    0−1=1 (carrying one 'two' from the left—then two minus
           one equals one)

Example:

Decimal			Binary					
150	1	0	0	1	0	1	1	0
108		1	1	0	1	1	0	0
carry 1	1	1	0	1				
42	0	0	1	0	1	0	1	0

Note a carry does not occur until the fourth pair of digits from the right when 1 is subtracted from 0. The fifth digit in the top row is brought into the fourth position where its value becomes 2. 1 from 2 equals 1, and the original 1 carried is added back below the line to the fifth position. With the sixth pair of digits the 1 has to be carried from the eighth position. It has a value of 2 in the seventh position one of which, on being carried, will also have a value of 2 in the sixth position.

Multiplication

This follows the normal pattern of multiplication for Decimal numbers although, in practice, since only 1 and 0 are involved, it means the addition of lines copied to give the correct place values.

Example:

Decimal				Binary					
45			1	0	1	1	0	1	
× 11	×			1	0	1	1		
450	1	0	1	1	0	1			
45	0	0	0	0	0	0			
		1	0	1	1	0	1		
495		1	0	1	1	0	1		
carry		1	1	1	1				
	1	1	1	1	0	1	1	1	1

Division

This again follows the pattern of normal Decimal division.

Example:

```
Decimal                        Binary
  13                               1  1  0  1
9)117            1  0  0  1)  1  1  1  0  1  0  1
  9                           1  0  0  1
 ___                          _____
 27                              1  0  1  1
 27                              1  0  0  1
 ___                             _____
  -                                 1  0  0  1
  ==                                1  0  0  1
                                    _____

                                    -  -  -  -
                                    =========
```

BINARY CODED DECIMAL

All of the Binary numbers so far used have been expressed as one continuous string of Binary digits or 'Bits'. This is generally referred to as 'Pure' Binary. However this is not the only way in which numbers can be stored in Binary form in a computer. Another method known as Binary Coded Decimal (BCD) consists of encoding in Binary each Decimal digit separately, using four Binary bits for each. Since there are only ten decimal digits, this gives a range of only ten different Binary patterns, a combination of which can be used to represent any Decimal number.

Decimal	Binary
1	0 0 0 1
2	0 0 1 0
3	0 0 1 1
4	0 1 0 0
5	0 1 0 1
6	0 1 1 0
7	0 1 1 1
8	1 0 0 0
9	1 0 0 1
0	0 0 0 0

Place values in powers of 10 can then be given to these Binary patterns depending on the position they hold within the Decimal expression.

C.A.—B

Example:
| Decimal: | | 4 | 6 | 9 | 5 |
Binary Coded Decimal: 0 1 0 0   0 1 1 0   1 0 0 1   0 1 0 1
Values: 4×10^3 6×10^2 9×10^1 5×10^0

EXPRESSION OF ALPHABETICAL CHARACTERS

In addition to numbers, the computer also has to cope with storing alphabetic characters and symbols. This means that each of these must be represented as a unique binary expression. There is no standard way of doing this in the sense that there is a coding common to all makes of computer but the following illustrates one approach to the problem.

The 26 alphabetic characters are divided into three groups of 9, 9, and 8 consisting of A to I, J to R and S to Z respectively. Four binary digits are used to indicate the place of the letter within the group, for instance A=0001 and I=1001 and these are prefixed with two additional digits to show the group in which the letter occurs, say 01 for the 1st. group A to I, 10 for the second J to S and 11 for the third S to Z. Thus A equals 010001 and Z 111000.

However, using a four digit group in which there are sixteen different alternatives, 0000—1111, to record only nine different characters and using a two digit group to record only three different groups out of a possible four is a very wasteful process. In effect we are using 6 binary digits with a total of 64 variations to record a range of only 26 characters. Assuming we wish to use a 64 character set, ten numbers 0—9, twenty-six letters, A to Z and 28 different symbols, the obvious thing to do is to divide these into four groups of 16 each, use the 16 codings 0000—1111 to record the position within the group and the four alternatives 00—11 to indicate the group. An example of a 64 character binary coding is given in the chapter on Central Processors.

EXERCISES CHAPTER 3

1.   Express the following Decimal numbers in Pure Binary.
      (a) 497   (e) 6·5
      (b) 226   (f) 17·25
      (c) 512   (g) 23·75
      (d) 127   (h) 64·375

2. Express the following Binary numbers in Decimal form.
   (a) 10001
   (b) 101011
   (c) 1111101
   (d) 110011
   (e) 10·1
   (f) 101·11
   (g) 111·001
   (h) 100·101

3. Express the following Decimal numbers in Binary Coded Decimal form.
   (a) 426
   (b) 814
   (c) 5865
   (d) 17893

4. Carry out the following additions in Binary.
   (a) 11101+10110
   (b) 1110110+111111
   (c) 10101+110011+11101
   (d) 111011+10110+11111

5. Carry out the following subtractions in Binary.
   (a) 11011−1010
   (b) 101010−1111
   (c) 1000100−101101
   (d) 1100110−11011

6. Make the following calculations in Binary.
   (a) 10101 × 11001
   (b) 11110 × 10110
   (c) 110101 × 101011
   (d) 11000011 ÷ 1111
   (e) 1011001101 ÷ 10011

4

Input Devices

In chapter 2 we saw that data, in its original form, cannot usually be fed straight into a computer. First it must be converted into a form that is 'machine acceptable.' This means that the data must be recorded on a medium that is physically acceptable, for example a card of standard size and thickness, or a paper tape of standard width. Secondly the mode in which the data is recorded must be recognisable to the machine. Broadly speaking Input data falls into the following groups:

(a) Where neither the original document is acceptable to the machine, nor the mode in which data is recorded. For example, a hand-written entry in a goods received book. In this case data must be transcribed onto a medium and into a form that is acceptable, such as punched cards or punched paper tape.

(b) Where the original document and the mode of recording are both machine acceptable. For example, data recorded in magnetic ink characters or optical characters on a document that the machine is able to handle.

(c) Where the original document is acceptable but the form of recording is not, involving a conversion to a machine-readable form using the same document. An example of this is Mark Sensing on Punched Cards.

(d) Where there is no need to use a document as such to record the data before transferring it to the computer but where data can be read in direct from a key-board machine, such as an Interrogating Typewriter or a Console Typewriter. We are now going to deal with these forms of computer input in greater detail.

PUNCHED CARDS

A Punched Card is a piece of high quality cardboard made to an exact size and standard thickness. The accuracy of its dimensions is critical for machine processing. Several sizes of card have been commonly used in the past but the two sizes in most general use

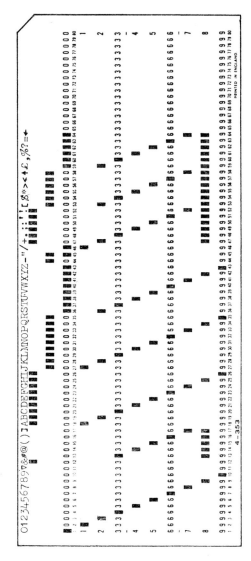

Fig. 4.1—80-col Punched Card.—With ICL 64 character card Code.
(International Computers Ltd.)

to-day are known as 40 column and 80 column cards. However, for computer input purposes, the most popular size is the 80 column card illustrated in fig. 4.1.

The card is divided into 80 vertical columns, each column having twelve positions into which holes may be punched. Each column on the card can record one character, a number, a letter or a symbol by means of a pattern of one, two or three holes unique to each character. These patterns of holes representing characters are known as a Punching Code. This code varies slightly from manufacturer to manufacturer.

For recording the digits 0 to 9, each is represented by a single hole in the relevant position in the column. For example, the figures 0—9 are punched into columns 1 to 10 in fig. 4.1.

Representing letters creates a little more difficulty since there are 26 in our alphabet but only twelve punching positions in each column. This problem is solved by dividing the alphabet into three groups of 9, 9 and 8 letters each. A—I, J—R and S—Z. The group in which the letter occurs is indicated in one of the three top punching positions, while the remaining nine positions show the numeric position of the letter within the group. For example, the letter D, the fourth letter in the first group, will be indicated by holes in the 10 and 4 positions on the card, the letter M, the fourth letter in the second group by 11 and 4. In the third group however, since there are only eight letters, the punching positions 2 to 9 are usually used. The coding for V, the fourth letter in the third group being 0 and 5. In the illustration the alphabet is punched into columns 18—43 in fig. 4.1.

Not only can numeric and alphabetical information be recorded but also a range of symbols each having its own unique pattern of holes. A number of these symbols are shown in columns 11—17 and 44—64 in fig. 4.1. An example of a complete 64-character Punching Code is given in fig. 4.2.

Cards may be designed to contain a single data record, these are known as 'Unit-record' or 'Single-record' cards, but on the other hand it may be more convenient to punch a number of records into the same card. When this is done the card is referred to as a 'Spread' or 'Multi-record' card.

If, for example, we want to record a customer's order for invoicing purposes, containing a number of items, one way would be to punch a separate card for each item, in which case we would have to repeat on each card the customer details for identification purposes. This would be a Unit-record card. If, however, having identified the

Fig. 4.2—I.C.L. 64 character card Punching Code. (International Computers Ltd.)

SYMBOL	CARD PUNCHING	SYMBOL	CARD PUNCHING	SYMBOL	CARD PUNCHING	SYMBOL	CARD PUNCHING
0	0	] RIGHT BRACKET	7/8	Q	11/8	' APOSTROPHE	10/6/8
1	1	A	10/1	R	11/9	! EXCLAMATION	10/7/8
2	2	B	10/2	S	0/2	[LEFT BRACKET	11/2/8
3	3	C	10/3	T	0/3	$ DOLLAR	11/3/8
4	4	D	10/4	U	0/4	* ASTERISK	11/4/8
5	5	E	10/5	V	0/5	> GREATER THAN	11/5/8
6	6	F	10/6	W	0/6	< LESS THAN	11/6/8
7	7	G	10/7	X	0/7	↑	11/7/8
8	8	H	10/8	Y	0/8	£ POUND	0/2/8
9	9	I	10/9	Z	0/9	, COMMA	0/3/8
SPACE	NONE	J	10/9	- MINUS HYPHEN	11	% PERCENTAGE	0/4/8
& AMPERSAND	10 OR 10/0	K	11/2	" QUOTES	11/0	? QUESTION	0/5/8
# NUMBER	3/8	L	11/3	/ SOLIDUS	0/1	= EQUALS	0/6/8
@	4/8	M	11/4	+ PLUS	10/2/8	↓	0/7/8
(LEFT PARENTHESIS	5/8	N	11/5	. STOP	10/3/8		
) RIGHT PARENTHESIS	6/8	O	11/6	; SEMI-COLON	10/4/8		
		P	11/7	: COLON	10/5/8		

customer on the card we listed across it a number of items, quoting for each one the Stock Reference number and the Quantity, this would be a 'Spread card'.

Now while this second method is more economic in that is reduces the number of cards used and saves repeating the customer details for each item, it does raise problems if we want to sort the cards into sequence. While it would be easy enough to sort them into customer account number sequence for, say, preparation of stores despatch instructions, it would be impossible to sort into stock reference number sequence for stock control purposes. An example of the use of Spread cards is given in the chapter on Applications.

In either case, cards are usually pre-printed to show the divisions between data fields with the content of the field shown at the top of the card. Fig. 4.3, illustrates an Invoicing Spread Card the first 22 columns being used to record Customer reference number, Order number and Date and the remainder of the card recording eight items by Item number and Quantity.

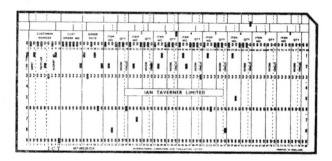

Fig. 4.3—Example of a 'Spread' Punched Card. (International Computers Ltd.)

PREPARATION OF PUNCHED CARDS

Cards may be prepared in a number of ways:

(a) By an operator reading the data from an original document, converting it into the required punching code and entering it through the keyboard of a card punch machine.

(b) On a Card Punch machine by reading data that has been recorded on the card itself in another form, (e.g. printing or hand-writing,) converting this into the required punching code and entering through a keyboard. These are known as Dual Purpose Cards.

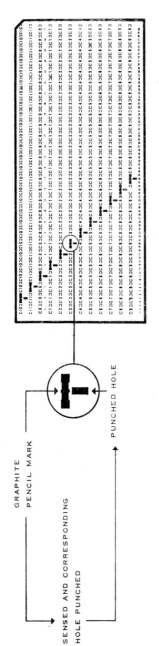

Fig. 4.4—A Mark Sensing Card. (International Computers Ltd.)

(c) By marking, at source, the position on a card where holes are to be punched in such a way that a machine will read the marks and punch holes automatically wherever the marks occur. This process is known as Mark Sensing.

(d) By punching cards automatically as a by-product of the operation of another machine, for example an Accounting Machine or a Typewriter.

(e) By a conversion process from Punched Paper Tape.

(f) By the computer itself as a form of output.

Card Punch

This machine consists essentially of a keyboard, a Hopper containing a supply of blank cards, a Punching Mechanism to perforate the cards and a Stacker to accept cards after they have been punched. The cards are automatically fed from the hopper, and progress column by column past a punching position where twelve punching knives are situated, one for each vertical position on the card. These knives cut holes in the card as information is entered on the keyboard. The card is then transferred to the stacker while a new card takes its place.

Keyboards are of two types. One contains keys representing the twelve punching positions on the card, and it is necessary for the operator to convert data on the source document to the relevant punching code before depressing the keys. The other type of keyboard contains keys for a full range of characters and the machine automatically makes the conversion to the punching code.

Dual Purpose Cards

While the same type of machine as outlined above is used for punching, the source data is written in ordinary characters in defined positions on the cards themselves rather than on separate documents. The data can be read by the operator and keyed in to the machine. It should be mentioned that when the card is moved from the hopper preparatory to being perforated, it still remains visible to the operator. Cards of this type are usually designed so that the written data will not be obliterated by the punching.

Mark Sensing

This again is a process of recording source data on the card instead of on a separate document, but this time instead of recording in normal characters the data is indicated by making a mark with a graphite pencil in the required position on the card as shown in illustration 4.4.

The cards are then passed through an automatic high speed punch which will 'sense' or 'read' the position of the marks and punch holes in the same places. While this method has the advantage of obviating the need to punch the card manually, in practice a major disadvantage is the limitation in the range of characters that can be conveniently marked. Since marking is usually carried out by laymen in this field, recording Gas or Electricity meter readings for example, marking is restricted to numerical information using only one mark per character.

Cards as a by-product of another Machine

In some procedures it is necessary to produce data in one form, say a printed Sales Statement for distribution to Customers, and in another form that will facilitate further processes such as an Analysis of Sales. It is often convenient to use machines that will produce the data in these two forms simultaneously. An example of this is an Accounting Machine printing a readable copy for distribution and at the same time producing Punched Cards containing elements of the same data that can be sorted and processed to provide additional information.

In addition to the above methods of preparing cards it is sometimes necessary to convert the input form from say Punched Paper Tape to Punched Cards. This can be done automatically by machine. Finally cards may be prepared as an output form by the computer, as discussed in the chapter on output.

ACCURACY OF PUNCHED CARDS

An essential of any input medium is the need for complete accuracy, otherwise the results obtained from processing will obviously be unreliable. In order to ensure the correct transcription of data from source documents to Punched Cards a process known as 'Verification' is carried out. The cards, having been punched once from the source documents by one operator are then passed to a second operator who punches them again from the same documents. If, on the second punching, a hole already exists in the position keyed-in, the card is released. If, however, no hole exists, it means that different characters have been punched by the two operators. The operator's attention is drawn to the difference, a check made to see which is correct and the card re-punched if necessary. It is important that cards re-punched to correct errors should in turn be verified to ensure the accuracy of the correction.

Different methods are, incidentally, used for verifying 80 and 40 column cards. The former uses an electrical sensing principle to see if a hole is present and the latter a method of altering the shape of the hole by converting the round hole produced by the original punching to an oval hole on verification. Test is then made for the presence of round holes which indicate error states. The basic principle of verification to ensure punching accuracy, however, applies equally to both.

PUNCHED CARD READING

The accuracy of the cards having been ensured, it is now necessary to transfer the data contained on them to the store of the computer. This is accomplished by a Card Reader which senses the pattern of holes in each column of the card, and converts these into a series of electronic pulses. The pulses are in turn either stored in Binary form in the computer's Central Processor or passed from the processor to some other form of storage device such as Magnetic Tape or Magnetic Disc.

The Card Reader consists of a hopper into which the cards are fed, a reading station, a mechanism for transferring cards through the machine, and a stacker into which cards are deposited after reading. The mechanics of card reading take two main forms. In the slower type of machine a number of brushes are suspended over a revolving drum, the card moves between the two and where there is a hole the brush penetrates the card making electrical contact with the drum. The machine can recognise the position and pattern of the brushes in which charges occur and translate this into the required pattern of pulses to indicate the character represented.

However, this method of reading, because of its mechanical mode of operation, is not fast enough for modern computers. In high speed readers, electro-mechanical brush sensing is replaced by photo-electric sensing, the card being passed between a light source and a row of photo-electric cells, one for each punching position on the card. Where there is a hole the light penetrates the card causing a charge to be set up in the cell corresponding to the position of the hole. Again, the position and pattern of the cells in which charges occur are recognised by the machine and translated into the appropriate electronic pulses for transmission to the store of the computer.

While the cards have already been verified to ensure that they have been correctly punched, an additional check is necessary in the Card Reader to guard against mis-reading. This is done by including a 'Checking Station' in the reader in addition to the Reading

Station. The checking station reads cards a second time during their progress through the machine, the data from each reading being compared before release to the computer store. One way of doing this is to add the number of holes in the card at the reading station and record this number in a register. The holes are then added again at the checking station and put into the same register as a minus quantity. If, at this point, the content of the register is zero the data from the card is transferred into storage, if not the card is rejected. Another method is to take the total of the values of the holes in to the register and to release the data in the same way if a zero total is obtained.

Card reading speeds vary from machine to machine from about 100 cards a minute in the older slower types of reader to more than 1,000 cards a minute in newer faster machines. An average reading rate would probably be in the neighbourhood of 700 cards a minute giving a maximum character reading rate of 1,000 characters a second.

PUNCHED PAPER TAPE

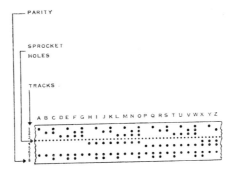

Fig. 4.5—Punched 8-track (7 data-bit) paper tape (International Computers Ltd.)

Punched Paper Tape is a continuous strip of paper tape on which data is recorded by punching holes across its width. Each row of holes represents a character (illustrated in fig. 4.5) the pattern for each character being unique. The number of holes that can be punched across the tape varies from system to system. 5-track tape, that is tape using a maximum of five holes to indicate a character, is 11/16th of an inch wide, and 6-, 7- and 8-track 1″ wide. However, most modern Paper Tape Readers use 7- or 8-track tape with a standard character code of 64 or 128 characters. The fig. 4.6 shows a complete 128 character punching code.

The number of tracks on a tape will determine the number of unique hole patterns that can be used to represent different characters. On 5-track tape this number is 32, and on 6-track tape 64. Since 32 different combinations of holes are insufficient for the range of characters needed, on 5-track tape, two characters are allocated the same hole pattern and a special 'shift' code inserted to indicate which character is meant. For instance, a number and a letter have the same punching code. To distinguish between them, before the code representing the number is punched into the tape a figure shift code is inserted, and before the same code representing a letter is punched, a letter shift code is inserted. The shift code need only be used when changing from one set of characters to the other. This problem does not arise on 6-track tape where 64 different hole patterns are available.

On 7- and 8-track tape, one track is used exclusively for checking purposes, leaving 6 and 7 tracks respectively for recording characters. Thus 7-track tape will accommodate 64 different characters, and 8-track tape 128. The track used for checking purposes is known as a 'Parity' track, and its purpose is to provide a further safeguard against errors caused by faulty transcription of data. A hole is punched in the parity track where necessary to ensure either that every complete pattern of holes consists of an odd number of holes (known as an 'odd parity check') or that every pattern consists of an even number of holes (an 'even parity check'). These parity holes are automatically inserted during the punching process. When the tape is being read, a check is made on each pattern to ensure that it conforms to the correct principle. If this is not so—if, for instance, a pattern with an even number of holes is found in a tape using the 'odd parity' check system—the presence of an error is signalled, and an investigation must be made.

PREPARATION OF PUNCHED PAPER TAPE

Paper Tape Punch

This is a keyboard machine in which blank paper tape is fed from a reel, through a punching position on to a take-up reel. The keyboard contains keys for the whole range of characters needed and, as each key is depressed, the machine automatically selects the correct pattern of holes to indicate a character and perforates the tape accordingly.

As in the case of Punched Cards, Punched Paper Tape can also be produced as a by-product of another machine, by a conversion process from Punched Cards and as an output form from the computer.

ACCURACY OF PUNCHED PAPER TAPE

Again it is essential that data recorded in Punched Paper Tape should be verified for accuracy before being read into a computer. Ways of ensuring this are:

(a) Call Over Method

This involves the use of a Tape Punch combined with a Printer. As data is punched into the tape a printed copy is made that can then be compared with the original document from which the punching was made. An obvious drawback of this method is that it is easy to overlook an error when checking by sight. It does not compare with a true machine verification of the type outlined below.

(b) Two-tape Method

This is probably the most widely-used form of verification. It involves two separate punchings by different operators from the same source documents. A tape is initially prepared by one operator on a tape punch and is then fed into a Tape Verifier. This consists of a tape reader, a tape punch and a keyboard. From the same source documents, a second operator punches another tape and as the characters are keyed in they are compared with the record on the first tape. If the two agree the tape is perforated and moves on to receive the next character, if not the key board will lock before punching the holes. The operator must then check back to the source document, locate the error and key in the correct character thus ensuring the accuracy of the second tape.

(c) Three-tape Method

This method, which is not often used in preparation of commercial data, involves the preparation of two tapes initially from the same source document by two different operators. The tapes are then read simultaneously into a verifier which compares character with character and where they agree automatically punches the same character into a third tape. Should the characters differ the machine will stop, allowing an operator to intervene, check the error back to the source document and key the correct version into the third tape.

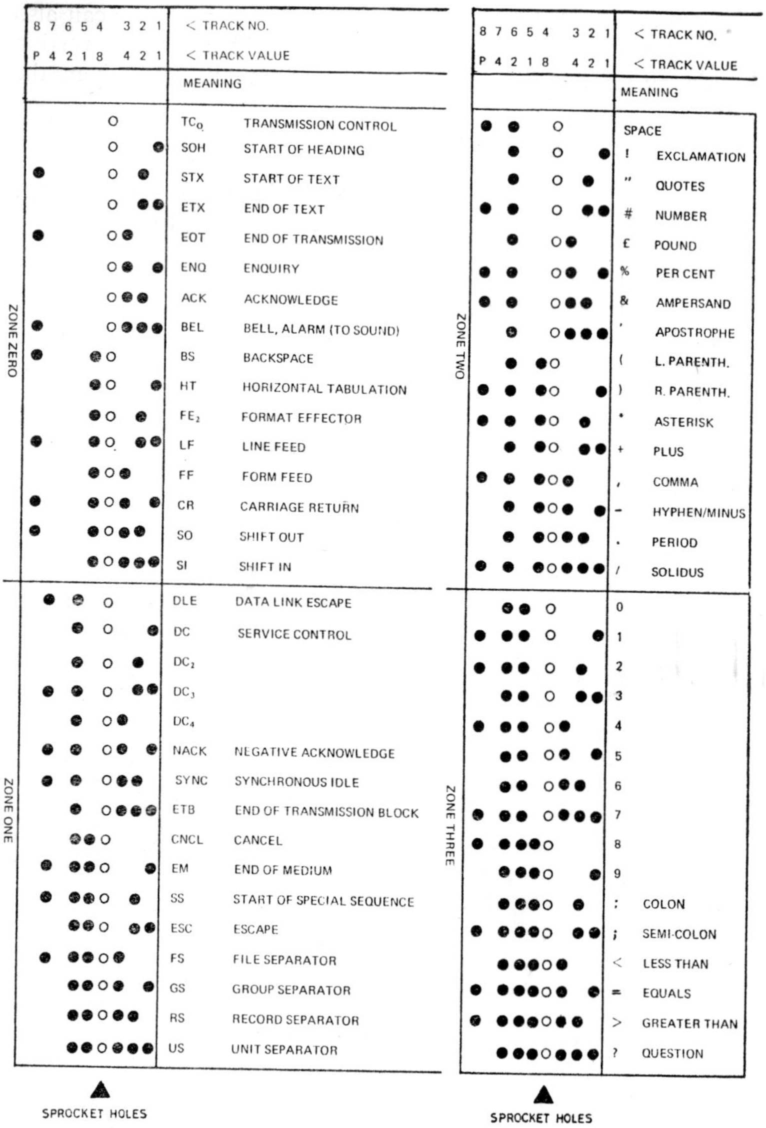

8 7 6 5 4 3 2 1	< TRACK NO.
P 4 2 1 8 4 2 1	< TRACK VALUE
	MEANING

ZONE ZERO

Code	Meaning
TC_0	TRANSMISSION CONTROL
SOH	START OF HEADING
STX	START OF TEXT
ETX	END OF TEXT
EOT	END OF TRANSMISSION
ENQ	ENQUIRY
ACK	ACKNOWLEDGE
BEL	BELL, ALARM (TO SOUND)
BS	BACKSPACE
HT	HORIZONTAL TABULATION
FE_2	FORMAT EFFECTOR
LF	LINE FEED
FF	FORM FEED
CR	CARRIAGE RETURN
SO	SHIFT OUT
SI	SHIFT IN

ZONE ONE

Code	Meaning
DLE	DATA LINK ESCAPE
DC	SERVICE CONTROL
DC_2	
DC_3	
DC_4	
NACK	NEGATIVE ACKNOWLEDGE
SYNC	SYNCHRONOUS IDLE
ETB	END OF TRANSMISSION BLOCK
CNCL	CANCEL
EM	END OF MEDIUM
SS	START OF SPECIAL SEQUENCE
ESC	ESCAPE
FS	FILE SEPARATOR
GS	GROUP SEPARATOR
RS	RECORD SEPARATOR
US	UNIT SEPARATOR

8 7 6 5 4 3 2 1	< TRACK NO.
P 4 2 1 8 4 2 1	< TRACK VALUE
	MEANING

ZONE TWO

Code	Meaning
	SPACE
!	EXCLAMATION
"	QUOTES
#	NUMBER
£	POUND
%	PER CENT
&	AMPERSAND
'	APOSTROPHE
(	L. PARENTH.
)	R. PARENTH.
*	ASTERISK
+	PLUS
,	COMMA
-	HYPHEN/MINUS
.	PERIOD
/	SOLIDUS

ZONE THREE

Code	Meaning
0	
1	
2	
3	
4	
5	
6	
7	
8	
9	
:	COLON
;	SEMI-COLON
<	LESS THAN
=	EQUALS
>	GREATER THAN
?	QUESTION

▲ SPROCKET HOLES   ▲ SPROCKET HOLES

Fig. 4.6—8-track (7 data bit) 128 Character Punching Code

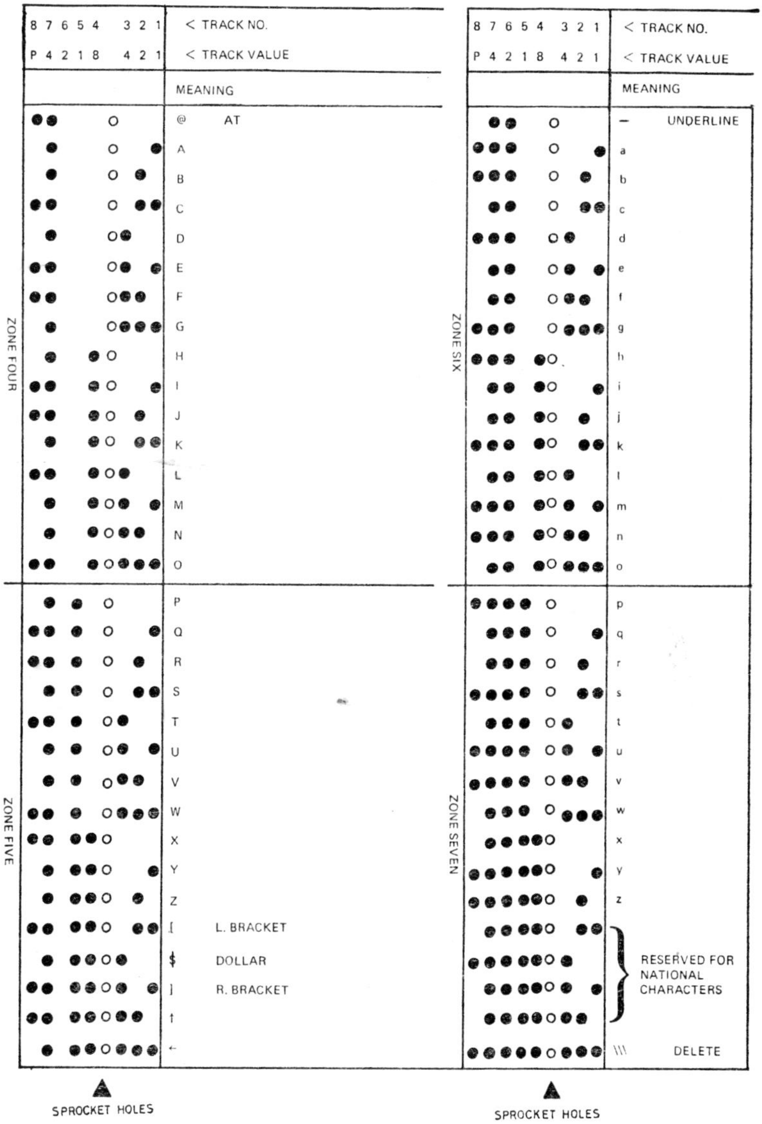

8 7 6 5 4 3 2 1	< TRACK NO.		8 7 6 5 4 3 2 1	< TRACK NO.
P 4 2 1 8 4 2 1	< TRACK VALUE		P 4 2 1 8 4 2 1	< TRACK VALUE
	MEANING			MEANING
	@ AT			— UNDERLINE
	A			a
	B			b
	C			c
	D			d
	E			e
	F			f
	G			g
	H			h
	I			i
	J			j
	K			k
	L			l
	M			m
	N			n
	O			o
	P			p
	Q			q
	R			r
	S			s
	T			t
	U			u
	V			v
	W			w
	X			x
	Y			y
	Z			z
	[L. BRACKET			} RESERVED FOR
	$ DOLLAR			NATIONAL
	] R. BRACKET			CHARACTERS
	↑			
	←			\\\ DELETE

ZONE FOUR / ZONE FIVE (left) — ZONE SIX / ZONE SEVEN (right)

SPROCKET HOLES   SPROCKET HOLES

Fig. 4.6 (*cont.*)

It was mentioned earlier that corrected errors in Punched Cards should themselves be verified in order to avoid errors occuring in the correction process. It is impractical to verify corrected errors in Punched Paper Tape in this way, but if these corrections are marked in some way on the tape they can be checked back visually.

PUNCHED PAPER TAPE READING

A Paper Tape Reader consists of a feed reel, a take-up reel to move the tape through the machine, and a Reading station. The method of reading is by photo-electric cells and a light source between which the tape passes. Charges are set up in the cells as light penetrates the tape.

Since the data is recorded continuously on the tape the computer must control the number of successive characters that are transferred to the computer store. This is in contrast to Punched Cards where each card contains a defined length data record. The number of characters that are transferred to the computer at any one time is known as a 'Block'. Block lengths, then, can be determined by programming or indicated by a special pattern of holes known as an 'End of Block Marker' or by a length of blank tape in between blocks.

In addition to these patterns of holes representing Markers, other patterns that do not represent characters may be punched into the tape. An example of this is a 'delete' code in which holes are punched in all tracks across the tape. The reading machine will ignore these patterns and will read valid codes only.

MODE OF RECORDING ON PUNCHED PAPER TAPE

In contrast to punched cards where each card usually represents a separate data record and fields occupy fixed positions on the card, recording on Punched Paper Tape is continuous and therefore there must be some way of showing where each field and record begins and ends. One way of doing this is to adopt much the same practice as with cards, that is fixing the maximum number of characters each field will contain and allocating this number of character positions on the tape. This method, however, can be wasteful. If, for example, a maximum field size of five characters is needed, giving a quantity up to 99,999, an actual quantity of, say, 56, would have to be preceded by three insignificant zeros, 00056. This type of recording on punched paper tape is known as a Fixed Field Length format. Another way is to vary the lengths of fields to suit the actual data to be punched but this means, of course, that fields must be separated by some kind of marker. In the above example, instead of five character positions, of which three are insignificant zeros, only three positions would be needed of which one would hold an End of Field marker. This is known as a Variable Field Length format. In practice it is found that some fields, by nature of the data, are of a fixed length, for example Account number or Stock Item number, while others are variable, Description, Quantity, Value etc. The use of a fixed field length for fixed length data imposes a validity check by ensuring that the correct number of characters are present in, say, an Account number. It is common practice to use both of these formats in order to combine the best features of each. This is known as a Fixed-variable Field Length format. Items containing a constant number of characters are treated as fixed length fields, and data items in which the number of characters vary, are treated as variable-length fields.

In modern Paper Tape Readers, reading speed is around 1,000 characters per second.

COMPARISONS BETWEEN PUNCHED CARDS AND PUNCHED PAPER TAPE

(a) *Speed of reading.* There is little to choose between the two. Tape, about 1,000 characters per second, Punched Cards 900—1,000.

(b) *Preparation.* Key operated punches used for both cards and tape. Use of full character key-board for paper tape eliminates the need for mental conversion to code. Cards can be mark sensed for automatic punching. Card verification more positive.

(c) *Cost.* While both punching and verifying processes use the same card, at least two separate tapes have to be prepared. However, volume for volume of data, punched paper tape is cheaper.

(d) *Flexibility.* Punched cards can be renewed, replaced and re-arranged in any required sequence. Tape is more rigid in that once it has been prepared the order of the data items cannot be altered and additions or deletions cannot easily be made. Cards, however, have fixed length fields. This is less flexible and more wasteful than the variable-length field facility offered by punched paper tape.

(*e*) *Security.*   While strict controls should be imposed on the use and storage of both forms of input, it is easier for a punched card to go astray than a section of a reel of punched tape.

MAGNETIC INK CHARACTER RECOGNITION (M.I.C.R.)

Preparation of Punched Cards and Punched Paper Tape for computer input usually involves two distinct stages:
(a) Preparation of a source document.
(b) Transfer of the data on to a card or a tape.
Use of M.I.C.R. seeks to cut these stages down to one by creating a source document that can also be used as an input form. Two conditions are necessary to accomplish this:
(a) The document itself must be machine acceptable.
(b) The data must be recorded in a machine readable form.
The system is based on the use of a stylised set of characters printed in an ink containing a ferro-magnetic substance. This ink can then be magnetised and subsequently detected and recognised by a machine.

The two most important founts at present in use are the E 13B and the C.M.C.7, the former originating in the U.S.A. and the latter of French origin. The E 13B fount seems to be the most generally used in this country while the C.M.C.7 fount is more widely used in European countries. Examples of these founts are given in Fig. 4.7.

The main development of M.I.C.R. using E 13B fount has been in the banking profession and the tendency has been to develop specialised machines to meet the needs of banking systems. However, a great deal of work is going on at the moment in the development of machines and techniques for wider applications. The use of M.I.C.R. in banking systems has been restricted to a range of 14 characters only, ten numerical digits and four symbols.

PREPARATION OF M.I.C.R. DOCUMENTS

Basic considerations in the preparation of M.I.C.R. documents are:
(a) Since the source document is also the input form, its size must fall within the tolerances imposed by the machine used for processing.
(b) The successful reading of the characters depends on the accurate reproduction of the character shape and constant ink density. This necessitates very high quality printing.
(c) The characters must appear in pre-determined positions on the

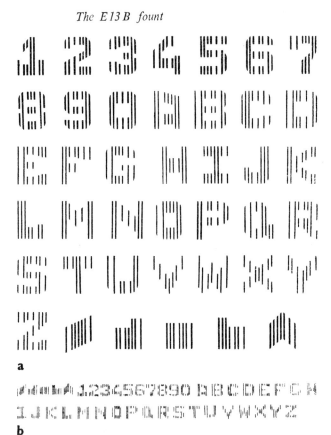

The E13B fount

The C.M.C. 7 fount

Fig. 4.7—Examples of Magnetic Ink Characters (International Computers Ltd.)

document to ensure their correct positioning at the reading head during processing.

There are two stages at which the magnetic ink characters may be encoded on the document. The first of these is after the document has been printed but before it is used. This necessarily is limited to non-variable data such as, in the case of cheques, the cheque number, the branch reference number and the customer account number. This is known as Pre-encoding.

The second stage occurs after the variable data has been entered which, in the case of cheques, would be after completion by the drawer. This is known as Post-encoding. The method used is to pass the cheques one by one through a key board machine where it remains visible while the operator reads the data and keys it in. The cheque then passes through the machine where the characters are printed in magnetic ink. As a precaution against error the machine adds the quantitative data and gives a total for a batch of documents at the end of a run. This can then be checked against a total prepared by pre-listing before the documents were processed.

M.I.C.R. READING

(a) The E 13*B fount.*

The ferro-magnetic content of the ink having been magnetised, the characters are passed over a reading head where the magnetism induces a current in the reading circuit. Since the induced current will be proportional to the magnetised area passing the head, a varying current will be produced determined by the shape of the character. By comparing the pattern of this current with standards in the machine circuitry, it can be recognised as representing a given character.

(b) The C.M.C.7 fount.

Each character is built up of seven lines so as to give spaces of different widths between any two lines. Recognition of the character is by coversion into a binary code in which a wide space represents a binary one and a narrow space a binary zero.

As was mentioned earlier, the main development in the use of M.I.C.R. has been for processing cheques. This entails two main functions, sorting the cheques into some pre-determined order, say branch order for distribution back to branches, and summarising the amounts on the cheques to give listings and control totals. These two operations are carried out on a M.I.C.R. Sorter/Reader. Speed of sorting and reading is round about 1,200 documents a minute, which, on a basis of a maximum of 75 characters on each cheque, gives a reading rate of 1,500 characters a second. While this compares favourably with Punched Card and Punched Paper Tape reading speeds, there can be a high rate of error rejection as verification of individual characters is not normally possible. This rejection rate was sometimes 2 per cent in early machines, although later developments have gone far to overcome this problem.

OPTICAL CHARACTER RECOGNITION (O.C.R.)

This is a second way of encoding data direct on to a source document using, this time, a character recognition process involving scanning by a light source rather than the magnetic properties of the printing ink.

The characters used are not as stylised as those required for M.I.C.R. and so are more easily read by human sight. An illustration of the N.2. Numeric fount is given in fig. 4.8.

$$1234567890-\times.$$
a

$$1234567890-\times.$$
b

Fig. 4.8—The N.2 Numeric Type Fount (Optical Character Reading) (International Computers Ltd.)

PREPARATION OF O.C.R. DOCUMENTS

The object is the same as that of using magnetic characters; to produce a document at source that is both machine acceptable and machine readable. The same considerations relating to document size, quality of printing and character positioning apply.

While, with the use of a numeric fount, values are determined by recognition of a character shape, an alternative way of using O.C.R. is by giving defined positions on the document a pre-determined value, and recording data by marking these positions in black ink or black pencil. The machine will detect these marks and assign to them the value determined by their position. A number of vertical columns of figures are printed, each with a dot immediately above and below it. These vertical columns are in turn divided into fields each containing one data item. Recording is by drawing a

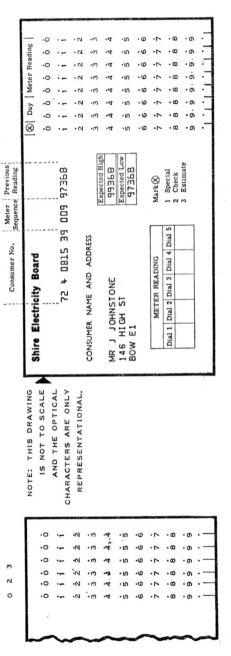

Fig. 4.9—O.C.R. Mark Reading Document (International Computers Ltd.)

vertical line through the character joining the two dots above and below. It should be noted that it is not necessary to print the vertical columns of figures in the special optical character fount, as it is not the shape of the character that determines the value but the position indicated by the mark. An example of an O.C.R. Mark-Reading Document is shown in Fig. 4.9.

Optical recognition characters may be inscribed on the documents in the following ways. Non-variable data may be included when the document is initially printed. Variable data is added by a keyboard machine or a mark sensing process. The line printer used for computer output may print characters which can be optically recognised by the input devices. Combinations of these methods may be used, for example in a meter reading system. Documents are prepared on the computer printer in O.C.R. characters, containing the customer's name and address, reference number, and the previous meter reading. The meter reader will enter the current reading in the mark reading area of the document which is then passed back through the computer system. The computer calculates the quantity used and prepares the bill together with a new document to be used at the next meter reading. In this example the document produced is both the output of, and the input form used by, the computer.

READING OF O.C.R. CHARACTERS

Optical characters and marks are both read by being scanned by an artificial light source.

(a) *Characters*

As each individual character is scanned, the reflected light is passed through a lens system and focused on a photo-electric cell. This produces a current from the cell which varies in proportion to the amount of light reflected from the dark and light areas of the character. The wave form representing this variable current, unique for each different character, is recognised by comparing it with standard patterns in the electronic circuitry of the machine.

(b) *Mark Reading*

There is a photo-electric cell for each position in the vertical column. The column is scanned from a light source and a mark in any particular position will trigger off a response in the appropriate cell. This is automatically converted into a series of binary pulses representing the value of the position marked.

As with M.I.C.R. one disadvantage of optical character recognition is that it is impossible to verify individual characters, therefore a fairly high error rate must be expected. Reading speed for O.C.R. documents is in the neighbourhood of 1,500 characters per second.

INTERROGATING TYPEWRITERS AND CONSOLES

All the input methods so far considered involve the use of documents in one form or another. In these cases data is prepared off-line to the computer, that is on some form of machine not actually linked to the computer, and then transferred to the computer store through an on-line machine such as a card reader or paper tape reader.

While this will be considered in more detail in a later chapter under the heading Data Transmission, it should be mentioned within the context of input devices that it is possible to communicate direct with the computer through the medium of a keyboard operated machine rather than going through the two-stage processes described above. It should be noted, however, that this is a very slow method of transferring data to and from the computer, the speed being limited to the rate at which an operator can depress the keys on a keyboard and the rate at which a machine can print out single characters one at a time. These are not more than about 5 and 10 characters per second respectively.

An Interrogating Typewriter is a machine linked on line to the computer that is used both as an input and output device to ask for, and to receive from the computer some specific item of information. For example, in a Sales Ledger system it may be necessary to know at very short notice for credit control purposes, the balance on a customer's account. The computer can then be instructed through the keyboard of the typewriter to look up this information and type it back into the machine.

In contrast to an interrogating typewriter which is used mainly for transferring data to and from the computer, a Console Typewriter is more concerned with actual operating procedures. It permits direct communication between the computer operator and the supervisory programme. By messages typed at the control console, the attention of the operator can be drawn to situations within the configuration needing operator intervention such as any mal-function in a peripheral or any unusual situation arising in the central processor.

While data communicated via the keyboard cannot be verified for accuracy, it will not be accepted if in incorrect format, and a message will be printed on the console indicating this.

Instructions to, and messages from the computer are typed out in plain language on a roll of paper fed through the machine. This provides a permanent record of all messages passed. Some consoles print messages originated by the computer in red, and those originated by the operator in black.

EXERCISES CHAPTER 4

1. Give an example of a simple paper tape code and explain with diagram how:
   (a) a character may be represented on paper tape
   (b) the number +324 may be represented on paper tape.
   Explain the purpose of a parity bit which may be included in a paper tape code.
   (Royal Society of Arts—Computer Appreciation Stage I)

2. Explain the safeguards that can be used in the preparation and processing of punched cards to ensure the accuracy of the data.

3. What do you understand by:
   (a) A Dual Purpose punched card.
   (b) A spread punched card.
   (c) Mark Sensing on punched cards.

4. Explain the methods that can be used to ensure the accuracy of data punched into punched paper tape.

5. Compare and contrast the use of M.I.C.R. and O.C.R. for recording data at source.

6. A data record consists of a number of data fields. How are fields and records distinguished from each other on punched paper tape and on punched cards? Distinguish between fixed and variable field lengths.

7. Describe an application in which you feel Optical Character recognition could be used with advantage.

8. (a) Describe and compare a simple paper tape code and a punched card code.
   (b) Either describe the process of recording information on paper tape or describe the process of recording information on punched cards.
   (Royal Society of Arts—Computer Appreciation Stage I)

9. As with punched cards, it is necessary to verify the data punched into paper tape before it is processed. Describe two of the main methods of verification.

(Institute of Data Processing)

10. What do you consider are the main advantages and disadvantages in the use of M.I.C.R. to record data compared with punched cards and punched paper tape?

5

Output Devices

In this chapter we shall describe and compare the various devices which may be connected to, or combined with, a computer to make the results of its operations available for use; that is to say, output devices. The data output from a computer can take three main forms. The first and most final form consists of sheets of paper printed with readable characters. It is prepared on a printer connected 'on-line' (i.e. directly) to the computer. The second form is a coded output, for example punched paper tape, which can subsequently be run through a teleprinter to produce printed reports. The third form is an output suitable for further computer processing such as an up-dated movement file on magnetic tape or summarised data on punched cards, both of which can form the input for further processing.

PRINTERS
There are three main types of printer: single character, line, and optical printers.

SINGLE CHARACTER PRINTERS
These machines print one character at a time in the same way as a typewriter. Depending on the type of work they are used for, they are known as Interrogating Typewriters, Console Typewriters or Teleprinters. While it is difficult to draw absolute lines of demarcation between their respective areas of work, we generally refer to interrogating typewriters as being concerned with the direct transmission of data between the central processor and remote access points. The use of a computer in this way usually involves what is known as 'real-time processing' which is considered in more detail in a later chapter. Console typewriters are used for operator control of computers and teleprinters for data-transmission 'off-line' (that is not directly connected to) the computer.

The maximum input rate of the single character printer is about five characters a second, and the maximum output about ten characters a second. This is too slow for use in the large-scale production of reports in data processing, but the uses of these printers will be considered later under the heading of data transmission.

LINE PRINTERS

The most important feature of a line printer is that instead of printing one character at a time it prints a whole line (known as a 'Print line') simultaneously. The two types of line printer most generally used for on-line computer work are known as Chain Printers and Barrel Printers. In these chain and barrel printers, which we shall discuss in detail later, the type faces move continuously even while the printing operation is being performed, whereas in the less-used Bar, Wheel and Stylus printers type faces remain stationary while the impression of the print line is made.

In bar printers, one bar is provided for each printing position in the print line. Each bar carries type faces representing the complete range of characters required. When in use, the bars are moved vertically through a distance which brings the required character into the printing position. Hammers are triggered off which strike the back of the bars and make an impression on the paper through a carbon ribbon. This principle is used extensively in Add-listing machines, Accounting machines and Punched Card Tabulators.

A wheel printer uses wheels with type faces embossed round their circumference. The wheels are mounted in a row, one for each position on the print line. Each wheel can be rotated independently to bring the required character into the correct printing position, and the whole row of wheels is then forced against the paper, making an impression through a carbon ribbon.

The principle of the stylus printer is that the impression on the page is produced not by a solid block of metal in the shape of the required character, but by the projecting ends of a number of wires carried in an open-ended box the size of one character. The position of the wires in each box can be varied to represent different characters, and with a number of these boxes arranged side by side along the length of the print line a complete row of characters can be printed at one time.

From a computer output point of view, the main drawback to bar and wheel printers is their slow printing rate, usually only 80 to 100 lines a minute. Stylus printers can print faster than this, but they have the disadvantage of being very complex and of printing a character made up of a series of dots rather than of continuous lines.

The printing mechanism in a chain printer consists of a closed metal loop or chain, which carries the type faces and revolves continuously parallel to the print line. Behind the paper is a row of hammers, released individually as the required character on the chain reaches the printing position. The speed of the hammer strike is such that a clear impression is made on the paper even though the type face is moving at high speed. To increase the speed of this type of printer, sets of characters can be repeated along the length of the chain.

A barrel printer, as illustrated in Fig. 5.1, makes use of the same principle of continuously moving type faces, but they are embossed on the surface of a metal cylinder or barrel. Each character is repeated along the length of the barrel, once for each printing position. (See fig. 5.2.) The barrel is revolved at high speed so that each character is presented to the print line in turn. When, for instance, the row of A's is lined up in the printing position, hammers are released simultaneously at all positions in the line where the letter A is required, impressing the paper against the type faces.

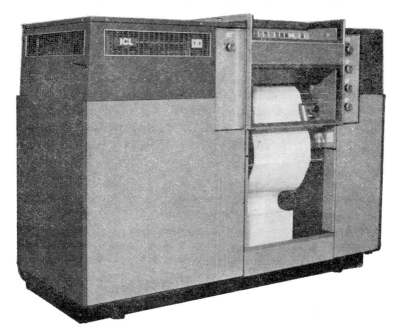

Fig. 5.1—A Line (Barrel) Printer (International Computers Ltd.)

Next the row of B's moves into position and these are printed, and so on through the whole range of characters impressed on the barrel. This means that a line of type is built up progressively, character by character, during one revolution of the barrel.

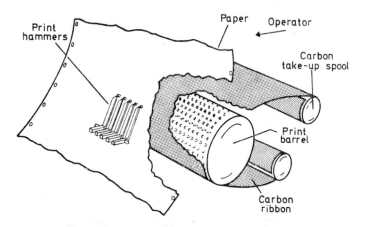

Fig. 5.2—General Arrangement of a Barrel Printer
(International Computers Ltd.)

Printing speeds of chain and barrel printers, while dependent to some extent on the number of characters in a print line and the number in a set of characters, are very high. Barrel printers, which are considered to be the faster, can reasonably be expected to produce 1,200 lines a minute, each of 120 characters.

The character set of a line printer usually has a maximum range of 64 different characters: 26 alphabetic, 10 numeric and the remainder symbols. (See Fig. 5.3.) The print line can consist of up to 160 character positions, although a line with 120 print positions appears to be the most popular.

The techniques for transferring and for controlling the transfer of data from the central processor to the printer naturally vary in computers of different makes and sizes, but the following general points can be made.

One area of store is usually reserved for output. In this area data representing one print line is assembled ready for transfer to the printer. If the printer has direct access to the output area of the processor, the transference of the print line will take the same time as its printing, since the characters are transferred successively.

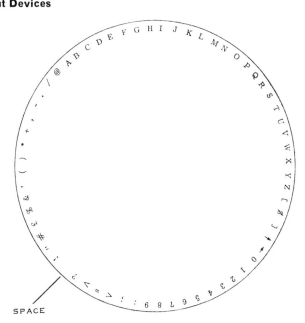

Fig. 5.3—Example of a Print Barrel Character Layout
(International Computers Ltd.)

This means that a great deal of processing time will be wasted while the program is concerned with supervising the transfer and printing of the output data. In the time taken to print one line—about 50 milliseconds—the processor could well perform thousands of operations. One extensively-used way of reducing the time wasted is to give the printer its own small store, known as a Buffer, to which a whole print line can be transferred in one go. The printer itself then takes over control of the printing operation, extracting characters from the buffer as they are required. This leaves the output area in the processor free to receive the next output record while the previous one is being printed, and also permits the performance of processing instructions while printing is taking place.

While the use of a buffer utilises processing time more efficiently, the fact remains that even with this provision data cannot be processed any faster than the rate at which the results can be output from the machine. In order, therefore, to make better use of processing time, output can be written on a magnetic tape, known as a Print Tape, when demand for computer time is heavy. This print

C.A.—C

tape will accept characters at a rate of up to 150,000 a second, compared with the 2,400 or so a second that the printer is able to deal with. The magnetic tape can then be printed out during a slack period.

GENERAL PRINTING CONSIDERATIONS

Further considerations in line printing concern the layout of printed data and the specification of the paper used. Continuous stationery is necessary for high speed line printing, sheets being separated from each other by a line of perforations across the paper. For many output reports pre-printed stationery is used. It is important that weight, maximum and minimum widths, length of sheets and sprocket hole spacing should conform with the specification issued by the computer manufacturer. Multiple copies may be obtained by the use of inter-leaved carbon paper or N.C.R. (no carbon required) paper, say up to six copies for the former and eight for the latter.

The arrangement and layout of data in printed form is subject to the following considerations:

(a) Printing time does not depend on the number of characters in a line but on the number of lines printed. It takes as long to print a line of two characters as it does a line of 120. It is an advantage, therefore, to get a maximum number of characters in a line by using stationery which is as wide as possible. If, however, the stationery must be narrow, consideration should be given to printing two forms simultaneously, side by side.

(b) Spacing a line, i.e. leaving a line blank, takes less time than printing a line, but the first in a succession of space lines takes longer than the others. It is, therefore, uneconomic to use too many single space lines.

(c) Wherever possible, in order to save printing time, all predetermined data such as the title of the form and headings of columns should be pre-printed.

(d) The assembling, layout and presentation of data for printing is subject to program control. This process is known as 'Editing'. This involves the insertion of symbols such as £ signs in the correct places, correct spacing of data items and arranging them appropriately to conform with the layout of the form used.

OPTICAL PRINTERS

These printers are in very limited use at the moment, line printers are far more popular in the large scale production of reports in data processing. However, the optical printer has advantages for some specialised applications.

A line of print is projected from a cathode ray tube on to a revolving drum with a light sensitive surface. As the drum turns, paper that is continuously in contact with part of the drum surface, moves in pace with it. Powder dusted on to the drum adheres to the areas covered by the projected image and is in turn transferred to the paper as the drum revolves. The powder is then 'fixed' to the paper by a heat process giving a permanent image, while the powder remaining on the drum is cleaned off ready to receive the next image. The whole process has similarities to the xerographic method of document reproduction, and its great advantage is that the shapes reproduced are not limited to a fixed set of characters as in a line printer. It can be used to print any diagram or chart that can be projected from a cathode ray tube.

PUNCHED CARDS

Card punches used for computer output are much the same in principle as those used for preparing cards for input. The mechanism consists of a hopper for blank cards, a punching station and stackers to receive punched cards, but there are in addition a reading station for checking purposes and circuits to convert the data from the form in which it is stored in the central processor to the appropriate punching code.

The Punching station consists of an arrangement of punch knives operated under program control. The number of knives used varies from machine to machine some having 12, that is one for each vertical punching position, some 80, one for each column, and some 960, one for each punching position on the card. After the card has been perforated, it is fed to a reading station where the data can be compared with the original data in the processor store. Should there be any difference the program may allow for a number of attempts to be made to obtain a correct punching, that is if the original stored data in the processor is still available to the punch. After say three attempts, the program may call for the machine to stop so that the operator can intervene.

As an output medium, punched cards are not very popular because of the relatively slow punching speed. While machines are available that will punch up to 400 cards a minute, many operate at the quite modest speed of 100–200 cards a minute. Even at 400 cards a minute this gives a maximum theoretical output rate of only 500 characters a second. However, in a small computer with limited storage capacity, punched cards may be the only way of storing data needed for future processing. This may be in summarised form such as carry-over balances, as a master file for the next run, or even data in detailed form requiring further stages of analysis.

PUNCHED PAPER TAPE

If anything, punched paper tape is a slower form of output than punched cards. While paper tape readers will operate at up to 1,000 characters a second most tape punching devices will only punch about 110 characters in the same time. Basically a punch consists of feed and take-up reels, a punching station and a checking device.

Punch knives are set up in the required position as data is transferred from the computer store and are then activated to perforate the holes in the tape. Before they reach the tape a signal indicating the pattern of knives so activated is sent back to the computer store to check the accuracy of the setting. Should there be any difference on comparison an error state is signalled before perforation occurs. Most punches are capable, on adjustment, of punching 5, 6, 7 or 8 track tape as required and they will automatically insert parity holes when appropriate.

Punched paper tape as an output medium does not lend itself to the requirements of large scale data processing where input and output volumes are large in comparison with the amount of processing to which the data is subjected. However, paper tape is often used in scientific and mathematical applications in which a small output is obtained from a comparatively small volume of input which has been extensively processed.

VISUAL DISPLAY UNITS

These units use cathode ray tubes, similar to those in television receivers, to visually communicate data held in the computer's store. Data may be projected on to the face of the tube in the form of numbers and letters, in diagrammatic or picture form, or in both forms combined. This is a very fast way of communicating information and while, in itself, it does not form a permanent record, the image can be photographed on 35 mm. film. Facilities are also available for the input and the manipulation of data by a device known as a 'Light Pen'. This can be used to manually direct the stream of electrons that form the image into any required pattern on the cathode ray tube. Alternatively it can be used to 'call-up' standard patterns and characters etc. for which the machine is programmed.

DIGITAL INCREMENT PLOTTERS

The object of this device is to communicate the output of a computer in printed graphical form such as diagrams, charts or line drawings. The machine basically consists of a drum which moves a sheet of paper backwards and forwards. To provide accurate positioning the paper is sprocket controlled. Suspended from a slide above the drum is a drawing pen that is able to move left or right across the width of the paper. This gives a movement in four basic directions, the paper backwards and forwards and the pen left and right. By altering the relative speeds of the paper and the pen, a line in any direction and of any curvature can be drawn on the paper. The machine is controlled by the program and the dimension and shape of the lines is determined by the output data. While programming for this type of output device is very complex and the output of data comparatively slow it is, never the less, a very fast method of producing output data directly in graphical form.

ANCILLARY MACHINES

Now we have surveyed the types of output device available, mention should be made of the ancillary machines that are often necessary to deal with output after it has been produced in printed form.

Bursters

Output from a line printer is in the form of continuous stationery with a line of perforations between sheets to enable them to be separated easily. Machines designed to pull the sheets apart, known as Bursters, operate by passing the paper over rollers running at different speeds so submitting the paper to sufficient tension to burst the line of perforations. They can usually be adjusted to take paper of various sizes and of varying strengths. An additional facility in many of these machines is the incorporation of cutting wheels to trim off the sprocket holes on each side of the paper.

Guillotines

These are used for cutting or trimming continuous stationery. They may be used in place of bursters by cutting either side of the row of perforations and are sometimes used in conjunction with bursters when, for instance, two reports are printed side by side and need separating by a cut down the centre of the paper.

Addressing Machines

In some computers there may be insufficient storage space available to retain all the names and addresses needed for distribution of reports. If this is so a separate addressing machine is sometimes used, addresses being allocated to the correct forms by comparison of reference numbers appearing on the form and also on the addressing plate.

Decollators

These separate multiple copies of continuous stationery from their inter-leaved carbon paper and are usually used before the bursting process. The machine removes the carbon paper from the copies by winding them on to separate rollers. If it is then necessary to re-assemble the copies, this can be done on a Recollator.

Folders and Mail Handling Equipment

Many output reports prepared on a line printer are in a finished form ready for distribution. An example of this is a Sales Ledger Statement ready for sending to the customer. After decollating and bursting the forms have to be folded and inserted into envelopes for distribution. Folding machines are available, but a more complex machine known as a Mail Handling Machine will cope with both folding and inserting into envelopes in one operation.

EXERCISES CHAPTER 5

1. Explain why, when using a line printer for output purposes, central processing time may be wasted, and suggest ways in which this can be reduced.

2. The output of a Sales Invoicing procedure consists of Invoices printed in triplicate on continuous stationery. The original is sent to the customer, the first copy to the Accounts office and the second copy to the Sales Office. Explain how ancillary machines could be used to help deal with the distribution of these documents.

3. Distinguish between a Single Character Printer and a Line Printer, giving examples of the use of each.

4. Explain the difference between a Visual Display Unit and an Optical Printer. How can permanent records be obtained in each case.

5. For what reasons would data be output in the form of punched cards or punched paper tape?

6. What do you understand by the term 'Buffer' used in connection with a line printer? What purpose does it serve?

6

The Central Processor

In an earlier chapter the Central Processor was described as being rather like the work area in a manual system into which source data is accepted and subjected to the processes necessary to achieve a required output. We saw that the functions of the central processor are, essentially, Storage, Arithmetic and Control. In this chapter each of these functions is dealt with in more detail. However, it must be said that it is impossible to talk of a 'typical' central processor because of the wide range of types and sizes available and the different methods of organising the processing functions. The following descriptions are, therefore, of a general nature.

STORAGE

One of the most significant characteristics of a computer, and one which distinguishes it from mechanical and electro-mechanical machines, is its capacity to store large volumes of data. However, it is not necessary or economic to store all this data in the central processor itself since other forms of storage are available outside the processor. All that the central processor need store at any one time is the data needed for immediate use. The rest is stored in one of the mass storage media described in the chapter on Storage, such as Magnetic Tape, Drums, Discs or Cards. For example, in a stock inventory system in which the stock balance for each item is to be adjusted for issues and receipts, the only data that need necessarily be stored in the processor is that relevant to the particular stock item being processed at the moment. Such a file could be processed by transferring data item by item between the external store and the central processor.

In practice, in order to get as much benefit as possible from the high working speed of the processor, as many data items as possible are transferred at one time from the external store, but the fact still remains that the bulk of the data is stored outside the central processor. A number of factors determine the size of the block of data transferred at one time (these are mentioned in the chapter on

Storage) but perhaps the most significant is the availability of space in the processor's store.

We said earlier that the processor need only store the information necessary for immediate use. This information takes two main forms. First the program or the section of the program that is required to control the work being performed currently in the processor and second, the data being processed. A simple analogy may help to clarify the central processor's functions—that of people going to the cinema. The queue waiting outside represents the mass of data records stored externally to the central processor. The number that can be conveniently accommodated at any one time are then counted off and allowed into the foyer. This represents the transfer of a block of records from the external store to the central processor. These people then pay their seat money one by one at a cash desk and a ticket is handed out according to a pre-determined routine. This represents the interaction of the program on the data records. Having paid their money and received a ticket the people move from the foyer to the auditorium, in the same way that having been processed the data is transferred to output. All the time this is going on, the manager is standing by to regulate the flow of people from the queue, to make sure the ticket issuing process goes on smoothly and, should anything go wrong, to get it rectified. This is rather like the control function in a central processor.

It should be emphasised that this analogy is only a simple basic parallel and does not apply in its entirety to every central processor function.

WHAT IS STORED IN THE CENTRAL PROCESSOR?

Program, Data and Control. These three factors must be present during processing. However, if we look more closely at the data, we will probably realise that it can take different forms. This can probably best be seen by considering an actual situation.

In a stock inventory system, concerned with keeping track of the number and value of spare parts held in a factory store, a record is kept which gives the stock situation for each item, under the following headings:

PART NUMBER	DESCRIPTION	UNIT PRICE	QUANTITY IN STOCK	VALUE OF STOCK

The record is made up of five data fields which are subject to varying

C.A.—C*

degrees of change. The Part Number and Description will probably remain constant all the time this particular item is stocked. The Unit Price is subject to occasional change as production costs or market prices fluctuate, and the Quantity and Value are subject to continual change as stock items are received into and issued from the factory stores.

Another way of looking at these five fields is to say that some are purely descriptive and as such are not subject to processing in the sense that they have to be changed or modified in any way. Others are quantitative and are subject to processing in the sense that the values and quantities need constant adjustment. This type of data is known as Master Data and reflects the up-to-date position of a particular activity.

Having said that these elements of master data are subject to change, obviously the change must be effected by the application of new data recording the detail giving rise to the change. In the above example the change in the master stock data would be brought about by the use of data which record the items received by, and issued from the factory stores. This data will be partly descriptive, to identify the master record to which they relate, and partly quantitative, to determine the extent of the change. Data of this type is usually known as Movement Data. Processing applies movement data to master data with the object of keeping the latter up-to-date. This is known as Up-dating master data.

The kinds of information stored in the central processor are:

(a) Master Data. This contains values that are continually changing and represent a current situation.

(b) Movement Data. This records changes that are applied to the master data to keep it up-to-date.

(c) Program. To specify the processing needs in the inter-action of (a) and (b).

HOW IS DATA STORED?

As far as the mechanics of storage are concerned, an account of these will be given in chapter 7. In most modern computers the Ferrite Ring type of store is used. Each ring is capable of being magnetised in one or other of two directions, and thus of indicating a Binary 1 or a Binary 0. In this section we are concerned with how data represented in this way is organised in the central processor store.

Each Ferrite Ring then, represents one binary character. This is the smallest indivisible unit of store and is known as a Binary Bit.

Furthermore, we have seen that each numeric or alphabetic character is represented in store by a group of these bits, each data field in turn is made up of a number of characters and each data record of a number of fields. All of this is represented in store in the form of binary bits. Now a store holding tens of thousands of these bits will be completely meaningless in terms of information unless we can define the beginning and end of each character, field and record. It would be rather like having a page of a book covered with completely random characters. Characters are meaningless unless they are marshalled into words, the words in turn arranged into sentences, and the start and finish of each sentence defined.

For example, unless we know the particular convention being employed, and where the characters begin and end, the binary number 10011110 could equally well represent 472, 916 or 158. As well as knowing what number a particular binary sequence represents, we have to know where in the store it can be found when it is needed.

Now at this point we should remember that there are in use many different types and makes of machine. There is no standard way of organising data in store that is common to all central processors, in fact the methods in use vary considerably. In view of this the following descriptions are intended only to reflect basic ideas.

We start off then with two main problems. (a) to define the size of each character, each data field, each data record and so on, and (b) to be able to locate any data item in store. One solution that may suggest itself is to mark in some way where each group of bits representing a character starts and finishes, but this is not quite as simple as it sounds. What kind of mark do we use? We only have two alternatives, 0 and 1, and these are both used to make up the character itself. We might reason, why not use a group of bits with a pattern distinct from any of those used to represent characters. Here again we run into trouble. Using this method we would probably finish up with markers so big that most of the storage space would be taken up with them. In any case it would be quite a problem to know where the marker ended and the character began. Since, also, we want to know the location of each data item in store, each separate bit would have to have a unique reference. With a store containing hundreds of thousands of bits this idea can be seen to be impractical.

Having discarded this, our thinking might suggest next that one way of getting round the problem would be to divide all the bits into groups of a standard size, each group containing sufficient bits to record one character. This fixes the limits of each group which means there is no longer a need to mark where each group starts and ends. In addition to this, there is no longer a need to give each bit a unique reference, all we need do is to provide a reference for each group. Now, although we have not solved all of the problems, we can begin to see in principle how the data is organised in the central processor store. It is rather like having a lot of small boxes, each having a reference number, as shown in fig. 6.1. Each box contains sufficient bits to record one character, and the character is located by the box number. The name given to this number is an Address.

Having decided to divide the store up into groups of bits, the next problem is to decide the size of the groups. Now we saw in the chapter on Binary that the number of bits required to store a decimal digit is four and the number to store an alphabetic character is six. Thus a 6 bit group would appear to be sufficient to hold any numeric or alphabetic character and, since with six bits we can get 64 different patterns, 000000–111111 (0 to 63), we could throw in a number of symbols as well, to give a range of 64 different characters. But now another complication arises. Suppose we want to store numbers as pure binary expressions? The biggest number we can represent with six bits is 63, seven bits are required up to 127, eight up to 255 and so on.

Now three points arise in relation to the storage of numbers in the processor. Firstly, storage in B.C.D. (binary coded decimal) form takes more space than in pure binary form. For example, 253 in pure binary takes 8 bits, 11111101, while in B.C.D. it takes 12. 0010 0101 0011. It is, therefore, more economic to store in pure binary. Secondly, calculations are more easily performed in pure binary, more complex electronics being required to handle arithmetic in B.C.D. form. Thirdly, as we saw earlier, numeric information may be descriptive or quantitative, the latter only being the subject of calculations. Descriptive data could well be mixed Alpha/Numeric, and so there is a good argument for storing this in B.C.D., but quantitative data is probably best stored in pure binary for the reasons indicated above.

We now have the situation that some data is best stored character by character in groups of, say, 6 bits, while other data is best stored in pure binary for which a 6 bit group is too small. One solution is to compromise between these two requirements by having a group that will contain an exact number of six bit characters and will, at the same time, be large enough to accommodate a reasonably large number expressed in pure binary. For example, we could have a group of 24 bits. This will contain either four 6 bit characters or

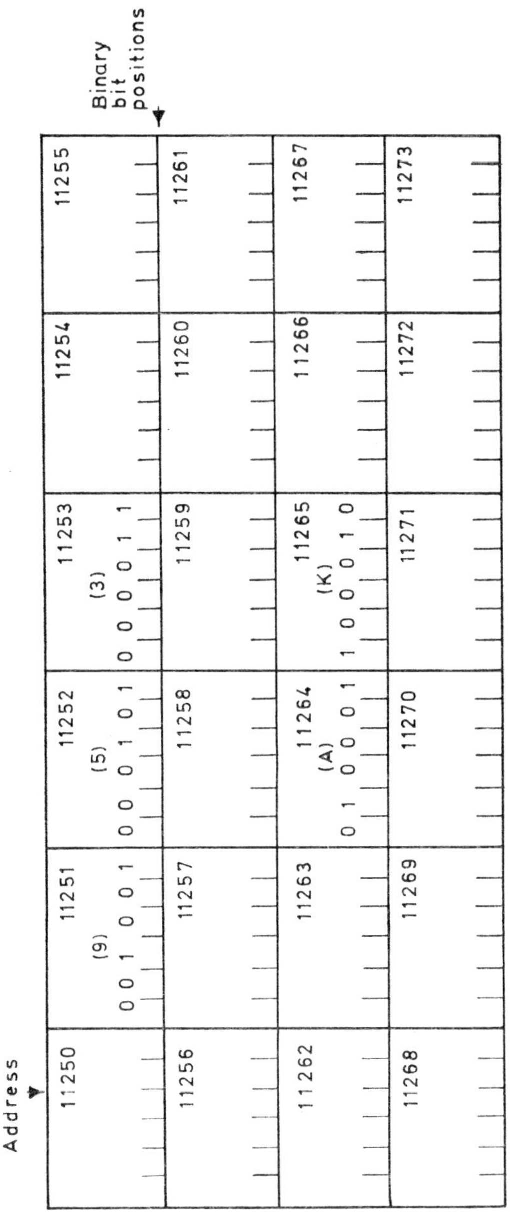

Binary bit positions

Address

11250	11251 (9) 0 0 1 0 0 1	11252 (5) 0 0 0 1 0 1	11253 (3) 0 0 0 0 1 1	11254	11255
11256	11257	11258	11259	11260	11261
11262	11263	11264 (A) 0 1 0 0 0 0 1	11265 (K) 1 0 0 1 0 1 1	11266	11267
11268	11269	11270	11271	11272	11273

Fig. 6.1—A Section of a Central Processor's Store. The number 9 is stored at address 11251. The letter K at address 11265

one pure binary expression. This arrangement, however, brings with it a further problem in that we can no longer give an individual address to each character within the group. But does this really matter? If the first character to be read always appears in the first position in a group and the succeeding characters are arranged in sequence, the machine need only refer to the address of the first character and keep on reading until instructed to stop. This can be done with a program instruction to read a defined number of characters, or by using one group of six bits to hold a special stop marker.

It would be as well, at this point, to attempt to organise our terminology. So far we have used the term 'group' to indicate a sub-division of the central processor store. We have suggested that such a group might well contain 24 bits, sufficient for four B.C.D. characters or for one pure binary expression. The name used for a group of this nature is a Word and a machine with a central processor sub-divided in this way is known as a Fixed Word Length machine. The sub-divisions of the word into character locations are often known as Bytes. Each word is addressable but individual characters are not. However, not all machines are organised in this way. Some adopt the principle mentioned earlier of having smaller sub-divisions, each holding one B.C.D. character only. This type of machine is usually known as a Character machine in which each individual character location has its own address. There is no reason why a pure binary expression, too large to be accommodated in a character position should not occupy a number of successive positions, the number varying with the size of the expression. This type of machine is often known as a Variable Word Length machine.

From this it may be inferred that in order to compare the capacities of central processor stores which are sometimes quoted in thousands of characters and sometimes in thousands of words, we must also know the number of characters each processor has in one word.

In suggesting above that a word might contain 24 bits and a character location or Byte contain 6, the only factor given consideration was the size of the binary expression. However, there are other things that have an influence in determining the word size.

Stored numbers may be either positive or negative, and a method must exist for distinguishing between these alternatives. This is usually done by reserving one bit in the word to indicate the sign, 0 equals plus and 1 equals minus. For example, in a 24 bit word, the left-most bit can be used for this purpose, leaving 23 bits to record the value of the expression, (see fig. 6.2). With numbers recorded in

B.C.D. form, the use of a 6 bit location leaves two spare bits, one of which can be used to indicate the sign.

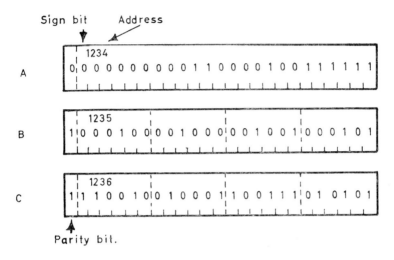

Fig. 6.2—Examples of a 25 bit word

A contains the pure binary equivalent of 24895. In the sign bit position 0 = positive, 1 = negative.

B contains the Binary Coded Decimal equivalent of 4895.

C contains the alphabetic characters TAPE.

We have already seen that the maximum number of different patterns available in a 6 bit group is 64. Should a wider range of characters be required, then more bits will be necessary. Some machines, for example, use a basic group of eight bits for each character. The recording mode used divides the character set into 10 zones, each zone containing 10 characters. The first four bits indicate the zone number and the second four the position of the letter within the group. An arrangement of this nature is known as a Zone/Numeric code. The first zone represented by 0000 contains the 10 numerals, 0–9, the second zone 0001 the letters A–J and so on. The code for the number 5 is 00000101 and for the letter H 00011000. In practice, to conserve storage space, the zone element of the codes for numerals can be discarded for processing purposes although the full Zone/Numeric code must be reassembled for output purposes.

While, as we saw earlier, calculations in the central processor are best done in pure binary, it is usual to simplify input and output procedures by reading in and storing data initially in B.C.D. form. When data is required for calculations, the binary coded decimal characters are converted within the machine to pure binary expressions and the results of the calculations converted back to B.C.D. for output purposes.

One further consideration arises in the storage of data in the processor. In order to provide a check on the accuracy of transferred data, additional space is provided in each word to hold a parity bit. A test is made on transfer of each word for an odd or an even number of bits, depending on the system used (see fig. 6.2).

WHERE IS DATA STORED?

In considering where data is stored in the central processor perhaps the short answer is 'Does it really matter?' In early machines it was necessary to keep a note of the address of each data item and to quote this in programming instructions. In modern machines the allocation of storage space is part of the control function of the central processor and if the processor itself records the location of each item there is really no need for the operator or programmer to know.

But for all this, specific storage locations may be reserved for specific purposes. Different types of machines use different approaches to storage, but generally, facilities exist within the processor for the following:

(a) Control. The control function is often stored in a number of locations reserved exclusively for this purpose. The address of these locations remain fixed.

(b) Accumulators. There are a number of locations reserved for holding data upon which arithmetic is being carried out.

(c) Data. By and large data may be stored anywhere in the processor's store. Usually, however, one part of the store is reserved for receiving and holding input data ready for processing while a second part is reserved for marshalling together and holding output data until it is transferred to the output peripheral.

(d) Program. Again, the list of instructions comprising the program can be stored in any part of the processor's store not being used for any other purpose providing these instructions are stored in the sequence that they will be worked through.

Of course there must be the facility for transferring data from one location to another within the processor. Data may be read to the reserved input area of store, transferred to the accumulator for arithmetic processing and the results transferred back to an output area. The remaining descriptive data in the input record is then transferred to the output area to assemble a complete up-dated output record.

Methods of transfer vary from one type of machine to another. In some machines data is transferred bit by bit until the whole expression has been moved, while in others all the bits in a word are transferred simultaneously to their new location. On the other hand transfer of an expression stored in B.C.D. form could well be done one character at a time. The first method is usually known as Serial transfer, the second as Parallel transfer and the third as Serial/Parallel transfer.

COMPUTER ARITHMETIC

However complex a mathematical problem, if it is capable of solution it can be solved by the application of the four basic rules of arithmetic; addition, multiplication, subtraction and division. In manual calculating, reducing a problem to these simple terms would be too lengthy a process and more advanced techniques are usually used to speed things up. However, a computer works so fast that it is easily able to cope with a mass of simple arithmetic in a very short space of time.

In fact we can make use of the computer's great speed to simplify the internal arithmetic processes even further. Multiplication can be performed by repeated addition, and division by repeated subtraction. In this way we have reduced our four necessary processes to two, but simplification can go even further. By employing a process known as 'complementary subtraction' we can deal with subtraction using additive methods. In decimal calculations, the complement of a number is that number which must be added to it to give a zero total. For example, the decimal complement of 429 is 571. When these are added, they give a sum of 1,000, in other words zeros in the three digits concerned. To subtract 429 from another number, say 760, by 'complementary' subtraction we add 571 to 760, giving 1,331, and as we did when finding the complement, ignore the most significant digit. This gives the correct answer of 331.

The usefulness of this method is that the complement of a number expressed in binary form is easily obtained by reversing all of the binary digits (that is each 0 becomes a 1 and each 1 a 0) and adding 1 to the result.

Here is an example of complementary subtraction, using numbers expressed in binary form.

110111—101101

Find the true complement of	1	0	1	1	0	1
reverse bits	0	1	0	0	1	0
add						1

	0	1	0	0	1	1 = True complement
	1	1	0	1	1	1
add true complement	0	1	0	0	1	1

110111—101101   =   (1) 0 0 1 0 1 0

In the computer store a negative number is stored in the form of its binary complement using the most significant bit in a word as a sign bit. For example, using a 12-bit word the number +52 is stored as

0 0 0 0 0 0 1 1 0 1 0 0

$\underbrace{\qquad}$ sign bit

while the number −52 is stored as

1 1 1 1 1 1 0 0 1 1 0 0

$\underbrace{\qquad}$ sign bit

Now if we wanted to work out 100−52 we would have:

100= 0 0 0 0 0 1 1 0 0 1 0 0
−52= 1 1 1 1 1 1 0 0 1 1 0 0

by adding (1) 0 0 0 0 0 0 1 1 0 0 0 0 = +48

Note that by adding in the sign bit the correct sign in the answer is obtained.

Since we can now produce the results of multiplication, division, addition and subtraction by forms of addition, all arithmetic processes in the computer can be reduced to the following four basic rules:

$$0+0=0$$
$$0+1=1$$
$$1+1=0 \text{ carry } 1$$
$$1+1+\text{carry } 1=1 \text{ carry } 1$$

The central processor contains special electronic circuits to carry out the arithmetic, known as Gates. When pulses representing binary digits are presented as input to a gate, a defined output results. The gates have names which depend on the output produced by a given input.

A two input 'OR' Gate has the property of producing an output pulse as a result of the application of one pulse to either input or simultaneously to both.

Input		Output
0+0	=	0
0+1	=	1
1+0	=	1
1+1	=	1

An 'AND' Gate will only produce an output pulse if input pulses are applied to both inputs simultaneously.

Input		Output
0+0	=	0
0+1	=	0
1+0	=	0
1+1	=	1

A third gate known as an 'EXCLUSIVE OR' Gate, is similar to an Or Gate but does not produce an output pulse when two inputs are simultaneously present.

Input		Output
0+0	=	0
0+1	=	1
1+0	=	1
1+1	=	0

THE ARITHMETIC UNIT

The use of a combination of these gates in an Arithmetic Unit will enable the four basic rules mentioned above to be carried out as illustrated in the following example. For this purpose we will assume that one set of gates is used for each bit position in the word, thus twelve sets of gates would be available for a twelve bit word. A set of gates for this example consists of two Exclusive Or and one And gate.

1. Input is applied simultaneously to the And gate and to the first Exclusive Or.

2. The output from the first Exclusive Or becomes one input for the second Exclusive Or.

3. Any output from the And gate is carried to the next set of gates as the second input to the second Exclusive Or gate and also as an additional third input to the And gate. This means an And gate that will give an output pulse if either two or three input pulses are present. (See fig. 6.3.)

Applying this the addition of 111100 and 101010 is shown in tabular form in figure 6.4 and in diagrammatic form in figure 6.5.

It must be emphasised that the above example is just one way, not the only way, of doing the arithmetic. Different machines use different arrangements of gates. Some machines use one set of gates only to process a binary expression bit by bit serially. In this case the output of the And gate is delayed one pulse in order to carry it into the next stage. Again, a combination of And and Or gates can be used, the output of the And gate being used to inhibit the Or gate output in the case of $1+1$ and also being used as the carry over to the next digit.

It is evident then, that a way of performing arithmetic is for the processor to pass the data through an Arithmetic Unit containing electronic gates. In many machines there are special storage locations, called Accumulators to which data on which arithmetic has to be performed is transferred and which hold the results of the calculations. For example, it is required to add factor A to factor B which are stored in locations 496 and 723 respectively. The program instructions will call for the contents of location 496 to be copied into the accumulator and then for the contents of location 723 to be added to the contents of the accumulator. Factor A, now in the accumulator and factor B from location 723 will now be circulated through the arithmetic unit and the sum moved into the accumulator to replace factor A. This total can then be transferred back to either of the original locations, moved to a completely new location or retained in the accumulator for further calculations. There are some machines, however, that do not use special accumulators as such but pass the data direct from the storage locations through the arithmetic unit, and feed the result back directly to the original location, obliterating or 'overwriting' the data previously held there. This mode of operation is known as 'Add to Storage'.

TABLE LOOK-UP ARITHMETIC

As an alternative to the Arithmetic unit described above, some machines use what is known as a 'Table Look-Up' principle for carrying out calculations. This consists of a number of reserved locations in store in which are kept the sum of, and the difference

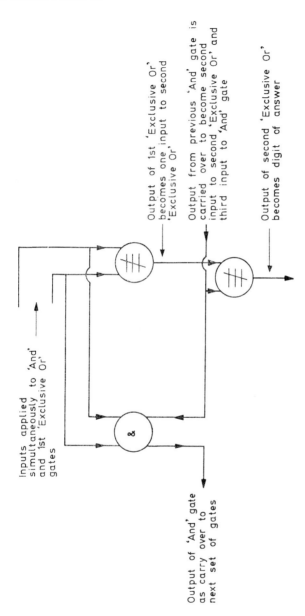

Inputs applied simultaneously to 'And' and 1st 'Exclusive Or' gates

Output of 'And' gate as carry over to next set of gates

Output of 1st 'Exclusive Or' becomes one input to second 'Exclusive Or'

Output from previous 'And' gate is carried over to become second input to second 'Exclusive Or' and third input to 'And' gate

Output of second 'Exclusive Or' becomes digit of answer

Fig. 6.3—A set of Adding Gates

| Bit Position | 'AND' Gate | | | | 1st 'EXCLUSIVE OR' Gate | | | 2nd 'EXCLUSIVE OR' Gate. | | |
	Input 1	Input 2	Input 3 (And output from previous stage)	Output	Input 1	Input 2	Output	Input 1 (from 1st Exclusive Or)	Input 2 (And output from previous stage)	Output
1	0	0	0	0	0	0	0	0	0	0
2	1	0	0	0	1	0	1	1	0	1
3	0	1	0	0	0	1	1	1	0	1
4	1	1	0	1	1	1	0	0	0	0
5	0	1	1	1	0	1	1	1	1	0
6	1	1	1	1	1	0	1	0	1	1
7	0	0	1	0	0	0	0	0	1	1

Fig. 6.4—The Addition of 111100 and 101010 using one 'And' and two 'Exclusive Or' Gates

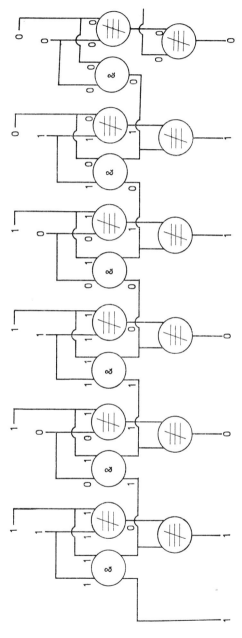

Fig. 6.5—A Series of six sets of Gates illustrating the addition of 111100 and 101010

between, every possible pair of decimal digits. The address of each location is determined by a combination of the two numbers to be added or subtracted. For example, to add 4 and 5, these two numbers would be copied from their locations in store into a special register where they would form the address 45. On reference to the location whose address is 45 it will be found that the content is 9, the answer to the sum of 4 and 5. Similarly the sum of 5 and 4 would be found in the address 54 whose content would also be 9.

To carry out subtraction, a set of difference tables are stored, addressable in the same way. The difference between 7 and 2 would be found in location 72. To distinguish between the addresses of locations containing the sums of numbers and the locations containing differences, a separate series of location addresses is used in each case. For instance, the sum of 7 and 2 might be found in location 0072 and the difference in location 0172.

To cope with the carry over from one digit to the next, one is added to the address containing the answer for the next pair of digits. To add 49 and 38 the sum of 9 and 8 is found in location 98 which is 7 carry 1. The 1 is added to the address formed by the next pair of digits 4 and 3 giving 43 plus 1. This is location 44 which contains 8.

One other essential function of the central processor is the ability to compare numbers and to take different courses of action depending on whether one number is greater than, less than or equal to another. One way of doing this is to load the first number into the accumulator and the second into a device known as a Comparator. The two numbers are then compared arithmetically and the result of the comparison placed in a register. The program then tests the contents of this register and the result determines the next sequence of instructions to be followed.

THE STORED PROGRAM

The series of instructions comprising a program is stored in addressable locations in the central processor in much the same way as data items are stored. Since the machine proceeds in sequence from one address to another when carrying out the program instructions, these instructions must be stored in the sequence they are required. This does not mean that they must be in one continuous sequence of addresses, but that there must be continuity between the last instruction in one series of locations and the first instruction in the next. For example, a program requiring 500 locations could have the first 200 instructions in addresses 1401 to 1600, followed by stored data in 1601 to 2000 and then the program instructions continuing in 2001 to 2300. The contents of address 1600, however, must direct the machine to 2001 for the next instruction.

Each stored instruction contains two basic factors. The first determines the operation to be carried out and is known as the Function, the second the location of the data upon which the instruction is to be performed, known as the Address.

A computer is required to carry out a number of different operations such as Add, Subtract, Read, Write. Each of these must be communicated to the machine in a form it will recognise and act upon. This list of instructions, known as a Machine Code consists, as far as the machine is concerned, of a series of distinct binary patterns, each one of which will cause the machine to perform a particular function. Machine codes differ from one machine to another but, in principle, contain these three classes of function.

1. Arithmetic instructions such as Add, Multiply, which process existing data in order to provide new information.

2. Instructions to operate peripherals, such as Read Card, or Print Line.

3. Data handling instructions involving the movement of data from one location to another in store, re-arrangement of data for output purposes or movement of data to an accumulator for calculating.

As its name implies, the address part of an instruction specifies the location of the data upon which the function is to be performed. However, in performing an operation on data more than one address is involved. For instance, if the function is Add then two items of data with separate addresses are required. Now in some machines only one address is quoted in each instruction. This is known as a Single-address format instruction.

In machines using an Add-to-Storage principle rather than transferring data to an accumulator a Two-address format instruction is used. This quotes the addresses of the two elements needed for calculating, the answer being over-written into the first of the two addresses. A Three-address format instruction quotes, in addition, the address in which the results of processing should be stored.

For example, if we had to perform the operation 'Add the contents of location 426 to the contents of 639 and record the result in 750,' instructions in the three different formats could well be as follows: Single-Address Format. (This would need three separate instructions.)

(a) Load the accumulator with the contents of 426.
(b) Add to the accumulator the contents of 639.
(c) Transfer the contents of the accumulator to 750.
Two-Address Format. (This would require two separate instructions.)
(a) Add the contents of location 426 to 639.
(b) Transfer the contents of location 426 to 750.
Three-Address Format. (One instruction only would be necessary.)
(a) Add the contents of 426 to 639 and record in 750.

Instructions in these forms, however, only relate to the data stored in the single locations quoted as addresses. More often than not a data item will occupy a number of consecutive locations. Indeed, in a character machine, one character only is stored at each address. To save repeating instructions for each location, a 'Count' specifying the number of locations occupied by the data item, is introduced into the instruction format. The instructions quote just the highest or the lowest address, depending on the system used.

The machine starts processing at this point and continues through the number of locations indicated by the count.

2501	2502	2503	2504	2505
	4	9	3	8
2506	2507	2508	2509	2510
2511	2512	2513	2514	2515
	3	5	7	9

Fig. 6.6—Two data items held in store

Fig. 6.6 illustrates the storage of the two data items, 4938 and 3579 in addresses 2502 to 2505, and 2512 to 2515 respectively. An Add instruction for these two items could read

ADD	2505	2515	4
(Function)	(1st address)	(2nd address)	(count)

By starting processing at address 2505 and 2515, working back through successive locations and decreasing the count by one as each location is dealt with, the completion of the instruction is indicated when the count reaches zero.

CONTROL

We have seen that the central processor performs a number of different functions such as accepting and storing input data, assembling and communicating output data, re-arranging data in store, and carrying out calculations, all of them specified by its particular machine code. Perhaps the most important feature of the processor is the control function which supervises all these processes and co-ordinates the activities of the configuration as a whole. Control instructions are stored in a number of locations reserved for this purpose, usually known as Control Registers. While the detail of the control function varies with the type of machine, the following factors are present.

Program Control

This is concerned with initiating the activities called for in the program instruction. As we have already seen, these instructions are stored in sequence in ordinary store locations. From there they are copied one at a time into a control register which is, basically, a multi-position switch. On recognising the function code, switches will set up the electronic circuits necessary to perform the function, and on reference to the address part of the instruction, will link these circuits to the appropriate locations. When the instruction contained in the register has been executed the next sequential instruction is copied in, over-writing the previous one, and this is executed in turn. In this way the program is worked through, alternating between the transfer of an instruction to a control register and its execution, until the final 'Stop' instruction is reached.

Input and Output Control

The activity of input and output peripherals is governed by the control function. In response to a 'Read' instruction the transfer of data from an input device is initiated. Checks will be made to ensure that the correct input device is being used and that the correct file is being read, and the control registers will set up a count to ensure that the required amount of data is transferred. It is also part of the control function to allocate unoccupied storage space to receive the data. In response to a 'Write' instruction, the control registers will arrange to assemble the output data in the required form, supervise its transfer to the output device and issue instructions to this device to accept and record the data.

A further and most important control function, is to identify and notify the operator of any mal-function arising in the configuration. In most modern machines these reports are communicated as typed messages on a control console typewriter.

Central processors work at a very high speed. The operation time of a modern processor is measured in millionths of a second which means that, in the space of one second the processor is able to carry out many thousand operations. However, a serious limiting factor in the speed at which a configuration can work, is the comparitively slow input and output rate. While it will take some 50 or 60 milli-seconds to read in data from one 80-col. punched card, the processing time to deal with this data could be in the order of only 2 or 3 milli-seconds. This means that the processor is waiting for most of the time for work to be getting on with and in the circumstances just mentioned, would be working at only about 5 per cent efficiency. One important aim in processing should be to make optimum use of central processing time by reading and writing data to and from it as fast as possible. One way of doing this, used very extensively, is to record all data on magnetic tape for both input and output purposes so increasing reading and writing rates to around 150,000 characters a second. This usually means that data must first be read from punched cards or paper tape to magnetic tape off-line and the output Print Tape also converted to print off-line. This method pre-supposes the availability of machine facilities for off-line working. However, transfer to the processor from magnetic tape still does not approximate to the speed at which the processor will work but it will increase efficiency to say 20–25 per cent.

MULTI-PROGRAMMING

The only way of using the central processor to anywhere near its full potential is by running a number of programs simultaneously. Machines, however, must be specially designed for multi-programming.

In a machine that can operate a number of programs at the same time, the control function is naturally more complicated than in a single program machine. It means that a number of activities belonging to different programs are going on simultaneously. In these circumstances an important element of the control function is to ensure that the processing facilities are used in the most efficient way. Each program is given a 'priority rating' which ensures that control gives the more important program preference when allocating peripherals and central processor time.

EXERCISES CHAPTER 6

1. Explain what is meant by the following terms:
   (a) Location
   (b) Address
   (c) Bit
   (d) Byte

2. Distinguish between a Word machine and a Character machine. Give examples of how data is stored in each case.

3. Explain the function of
   (a) the core store
   (b) the accumulator
   (c) the arithmetic unit.

   (Royal Society of Arts—Computer Appreciation—Stage I)

   Outline in detail how information is held in core store.

4. Explain the methods that can be used to increase the efficiency of the usage of central processor time.

5. Outline the main functions of a control unit.

6. Explain how negative numbers can be stored in a central processor. Using a 12-bit word, illustrate the storage of (a) a positive number and (b) a negative number.

7. What do you understand by 'Master Data' and 'Movement Data'. Using any system of your choice, give an example of each type of data.

8. Explain how the program is stored in the central processor and describe the routine for carrying out the instructions.

9. What do you understand by 'Table Look-up'. Describe how this device works.

10. What are the main classes of instructions found in a machine code. Give examples of these.

11. What is meant by an instruction written in Three-address format. Suggest other ways of writing instructions and give examples of each.

12. Write a list of instructions, using a Single-Address format for adding two numbers and subtracting the total from a third. The result is to be stored in the location of the first number. Use imaginary addresses.

13. Describe briefly the work of a central processor mentioning its main functions.

14. Show diagrammatically how binary addition can be accomplished with the use of 'And' and 'Or' gates.

7

Computer Storage

It has already been shown that one of the fundamental characteristics of a computer is its capacity to store large quantities of information, including not only the data involved in a procedure, but also the program necessary to carry it out.

In large scale data processing, the volume of facts and figures involved is often so great that it would be impractical to have a Central Processor capable of storing all of them. Take as an example a simple Sales Ledger Posting system with five thousand customer accounts. Each account would record initially the Customer name and address, the account number and an opening balance. Postings would then be made to these accounts from Invoices for goods sold, Credit Notes for goods returned, and for Cash received. The data on each account could well comprise upwards of 100 characters, making over 500,000 characters for the file as a whole. It would need quite a large and expensive processor to store this quantity of data in addition to the program for processing it. Indeed, it would be unnecessary, since the processor will only be concerned with that section of the data on which it is currently working. Provided that all the data is quickly accessible, there is no need for the whole of it to be stored in the processor itself.

In order to see how computer data storage can be most economically arranged, it will be helpful to consider first how a Sales Ledger system of the above kind would be operated using keyboard accounting machines.

We would have a file of Sales Ledger cards, probably in numerical or alphabetical order, and a file of Sales Invoices in the same order for posting to the Ledger cards. The card with the reference number or name corresponding with the top invoice would be selected and inserted into the machine. The data would then be read from the invoice and posted to the card through the machine keyboard, the machine automatically calculating and printing a revised balance on the card. The whole operation would be guided by a program built into the machine. The posting to one card having been completed, it

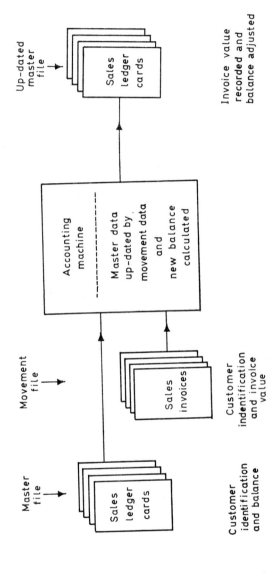

Fig. 7.1—Up-dating Sales Ledger Cards by Sales Invoices

would be returned to the file and the operation repeated for the next card and invoice until, finally, the whole file had been dealt with. (See fig. 7.1.)

During the processing run the accounting machine only contains detailed data relating to the account it is immediately processing. It accepts data for that one account from the two files, processes it and returns the up dated card to the file before accepting further data for the next account.

Similarly, in the case of a computer, files of data can be kept external to the processor. Information is read in from these files as it is required, processed, the results returned to the file and the process repeated for the next section of data. When the posting run is completed the 'up dated' data is now stored in a file external to the processor and the processor's store is now 'empty' ready to accept data for another system.

The kinds of storage can, therefore, be divided into:

(a) INTERNAL STORAGE, i.e. storage within the central processor, and

(b) EXTERNAL STORAGE or BACKING STORAGE which exists outside the processor but is accessible by the processor when required.

INTERNAL STORAGE

MAGNETIC DRUMS

This form of storage was used in most early central processors. It consists of a non-magnetic metal cylinder with a magnetisable coating on its outer surface. This surface is divided into a number of parallel tracks and each track is in turn divided into a number of sections each section recording one word or character in binary form (see fig. 7.2). Density of the tracks is in the region of 30 per inch along the width of the drum and the density of the binary bits up to 100 per inch along the length of each track. Recording is through heads, located one above each track, which magnetise spots along the track to indicate binary bits. One spot equals a binary 1, no spot equals 0. Heads are used for both reading and writing to the drum. Since it would be impossible to mount 30 heads in the space of one inch, these are usually staggered around the periphery of the drum.

Each location is addressable by reference to the track in which it is situated and its position on the track. The drum revolves at high

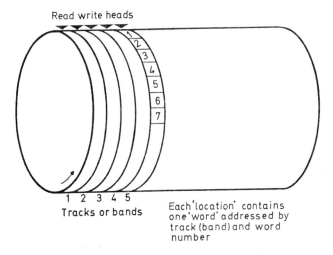

Read write heads

1 2 3 4 5
Tracks or bands

Each 'location' contains
one 'word' addressed by
track (band) and word
number

Fig. 7.2—Diagrammatic representation of drum storage (International Computers Ltd.)

speed under the fixed heads so that each location will pass under a head once in every revolution. The capacity of the drum will, of course, vary with its size, but to give some idea, a small drum will contain some 128 tracks each with space for 1,025 locations giving a total capacity of 132,072 characters.

One major disadvantage in the use of magnetic drums is that, while there is instantaneous reference to any one track through its individual read/write head, reference to any particular location is delayed while the drum revolves until the location appears under the head. As a result, for a drum revolving at 3,000 revolutions a minute, reference to data that had just passed under a head would require the drum to complete nearly a whole revolution taking almost 20 milli-seconds. Even if the average distance of any location from the read/write head is taken as one-half the circumference of the drum, the average access time is still 10 milli-seconds. Since a modern computer will complete an operation in a few millionths of a second and be instantly ready to proceed to the next stage, this delay of 10 milli-seconds is too long to be economically acceptable.

True, the delay can be minimised by a technique known as Program Optimisation. This arranges for each item of data to be placed in the location that is about to pass under a head at the moment it is required. This technique, however, involves very complex and laborious programming.

While modern drum facilities are much improved, with storage capacities up to 8,000,000 characters and an access time of a few thousanths of a second, this speed is still insufficient for their use as an immediate access store in a central processor. Drum storage is more generally used nowadays as a form of external or backing store.

The long access time of early forms of drum storage led to the development of ferro-magnetic rings as a more generally acceptable form of storage, overcoming the delay and enabling programming to be simplified.

FERRITE CORE STORE

The basic principle of this form of storage is to use small Ferrite rings, known as Cores, 12/1,000ths—50/1,000ths inch outside diameter, which can be magnetised in either of two directions and can thus represent a binary 0 or a binary 1. By passing an electric current in the appropriate direction along a wire or wires threaded through a core, the north seeking ends of the particles of ferrite making up the core can be made to point in a clockwise or anti-clockwise direction.

A number of these ferrite cores are arranged in a square (see fig. 7.3) each line of cores being threaded by wires in two directions at right angles to each other. We then have the situation that only one core lies at the intersection of any two wires. The current required to alter the direction of the magnetism in a core must be of a minimum critical value, thus if currents of one half of this value are passed through two wires at right angles to each other this critical minimum will only be located where the two wires intersect. That is, at this point the sum of the two half pulses is sufficient to change the condition of the core, but at this point only. This means that any individual core in the square, or matrix as it is usually called, can be selected according to its unique reference on the grid of wires.

However, in one matrix, or plane, only one core can be accessed at a time. If, for example, attempt was made to access two cores through two wires in each direction, since these intersect at four points, four, not two, cores would be effected.

To enable access to a number of cores to be made simultaneously a number of planes are assembled vertically thus giving a number of vertical columns of cores. Each core in a column represents a binary bit and the column a binary word. All of the cores in a selected column can be accessed simultaneously by passing pulses through the appropriate pair of wires in each plane at the same time. (See fig. 7.4.)

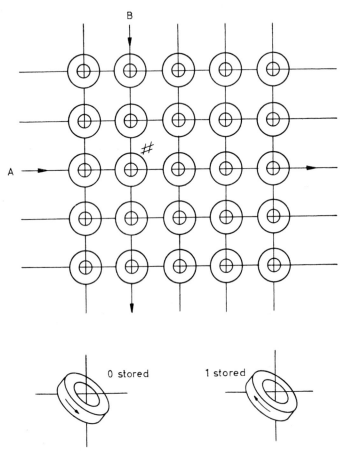

Fig. 7.3—Section of a Magnetic Core Store Matrix

To change the state of core currents of equal strength are sent simultaneously through wires A and B. The amplitude of a single pulse is insufficient to change the state of any core but at the point of coincidence the sum of currents A and B is sufficient to change that core's magnetic state

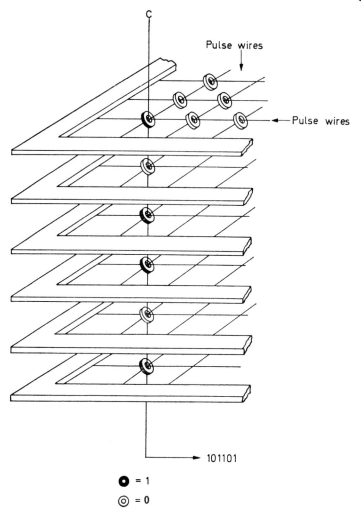

Fig. 7.4—Showing 3-dimensional section of a Core Store with 6 planes. Each vertical column of cores represents one 6-bit word which can be read by sense wire 'C'

In addition to the two wires already mentioned, a third, a sense wire, is threaded through the cores for reading purposes. In order to read a word, the first two wires are pulsed with a current to set all of the cores in the word to zeros. Where a core indicates one, the reversal induces a pulse in the sense wire which is in turn used to set the corresponding bit in a special register to 1. This means, after reading a word, all of the cores are set at zero, but normally it will be required to retain the information originally represented, which means it must now be re-written back to the original position. This is done immediately and automatically by copying back from the special register now containing the word. This is known as a read/write cycle and the time taken to do this is known as the cycle time for the store. While this time differs from machine to machine it is usually measured in millionths of a second although in very modern machines this time is quoted in nano-seconds i.e. thousandths of millionths of a second.

Ferrite Core stores of this nature, involving the wiring of many thousand rings, are very expensive to produce and it is sound practice therefore, to keep the size of the store as small as possible while still enabling the computer to do its job effectively. For operations needing storage facilities greater than the capacity of the internal Ferrite Core store, use is made of backing stores external to the processor.

Store sizes are quoted in terms of so many thousand words or characters of store space, the symbol K being used to denote 1,024. For example a 16K store has 16,384 locations.

Since access to this form of store is not dependent upon a mechanical operation as with revolving drums, access time to every location is virtually identical. The main limiting factor is the rate at which a current will pass through a wire, and to decrease access time the tendency is to manufacture smaller components and so shorten the distance over which the current has to pass.

EXTERNAL STORAGE

As was indicated earlier, the internal store of a computer is kept as small as possible compatible with the efficient working of the machine. Its capacity would normally be insufficient to store all of the information required in processing an average business system. Since only a small proportion of the information is required at any one time, it is practical to have this mass of data stored external to the processor. This form of storage is usually known as BACKING storage.

There are basically two kinds of backing store called Serial Access and Random Access. The difference between these hinges on the way in which data can be located when required. To illustrate this, if we had half-a-dozen table tennis balls stored in a long square-sectioned box, two of the ways in which the balls could be got out are:
1. Through a lid at the end, or
2. Through a lid on one side down the full length of the box.

In the first case, if we wanted to get at the third ball it would be necessary to remove the first two before it became accessible. This is an example of SERIAL access storage. In order to reach one particular item of data in serial access storage it is necessary to run through all the items of data preceding it.

In the second case we could gain access to the third ball without disturbing the others since they appear all laid out in a row. This is an example of the type of storage known as RANDOM ACCESS or DIRECT ACCESS. Data in random access storage is 'laid out' in such a way that any item can be selected without reference to the others.

Of the various types of External or Backing storage some are Serial Access and some are Random or Direct Access.

Magnetic Tape	
Punched Cards	Serial Access Stores
Punched Paper Tape	
Magnetic Drums	
Magnetic Discs	Random Access Stores
Magnetic Cards	

The obvious advantage in the use of random access storage is, of course, the increased speed with which any particular item of data can be located. However, it must be remembered, that random access has not necessarily an advantage in speed if data stored sequentially on Magnetic Tape is used in the same order.

SERIAL ACCESS STORES

Punched Cards

As we saw earlier, one of the main ways of recording data for computer processing is in the form of holes punched into cards. A collection of these cards containing data relating to an aspect of a particular system we call a Punched Card File, that is, it is a store of data in punched card form. Now it would be possible to store all of the data, both input and output, in this form. However, this would be very wasteful of computer time, as the effective reading rate is only about 60,000 characters a minute and the output rate appreciably less than one-half of this. A more usual and more economical method would be to transfer the data from the cards to a form of storage with a much faster transfer rate, say magnetic tape and use this for the on-line processing.

Other disadvantages of cards as mass storage media are:
(a) The limited amount of data that can be recorded on a single card, a maximum of 80 characters.
(b) The vast number of cards necessary to store large volumes of data with the attendant storage and handling difficulties.
(c) While cards may be pre-sorted by machine to any required order, they can still only be processed serially, one card at a time in order.
(d) Problems of security. With a very large number of cards it is possible for some to go astray.

Punched Paper Tape

The transfer rate from punch paper tape to the processor is fairly slow, as with punched cards. It is not considered suitable for large scale storage and again it is usual to transfer the data to a form of storage having a much faster access time. Tape reading speed in the neighbourhood of 1,000 characters per second and output speed of 110 characters per second can, indeed, impose severe restrictions on the processing speed of the computer. While punched paper tape does not present such acute storage and handling problems as cards, (a great deal of data can be stored on one spool of paper tape) it is less flexible. Once the tape has been prepared the order in which the data items appear must remain unchanged. Unlike punched cards it cannot be sorted to another sequence.

Magnetic Tape

Magnetic Tape is a very convenient way of storing large volumes of data in a comparatively small space. Magnetic Tape Decks are linked permanently to the computer but the reels of tape are interchangeable. This means that a library of tapes can be built up containing stored data, and selected and loaded on to a deck for processing as and when required. Data items recorded on magnetic tape can only be serially accessed by the computer. As it is impractical for the computer to jump from one location to another on the tape in order to find a required data item, it must progress serially through the tape, rejecting irrelevant data, until it finds the item required. This form of storage then is used for data which is to be processed in the same sequence as it appears on the tape.

Important characteristics of magnetic tape are:

(a) Several million characters can be held on one tape.

(b) Reels of tape can be used repeatedly by erasing data no longer required and recording new data.

(c) Data can be read from and written to the tape at high speed, up to about 150,000 characters a second.

(d) Data may be preserved for an indefinite length of time until deliberately erased.

(e) Unlike punched cards, the record length can be variable.

Magnetic Tape, usually $\frac{1}{4}''$ to $1''$ wide is made of a plastic material coated on one side with a magnetisable substance. Length of reels varies from 1,200 to 3,600 feet.

The tape deck is in some ways similar to a domestic tape recorder. It has three main elements: (see fig. 7.5)

1. A recording, reading and erasing device.

2. A driving mechanism to move the tape past the read/write head.

3. Two reels, one holding the unprocessed tape and the other to take up the processed tape.

On either side of the read/write head are loops or reservoirs of tape which help to ensure that the tape passes the head at a constant speed. In some tape decks three heads are used, one for reading, one for writing and the third for erasing. Other decks have two heads, the write and erase functions being combined. Irrespective of the design of the machine these three basic functions are necessary, reading, writing and erasing.

Characters are recorded by the recording head creating magnetic patterns on the surface of the tape. Depending on the width of the tape used, these patterns may be recorded along the length of the tape or across its face. Most modern machines use a recording mode very similar to punched paper tape, in which the tape is divided into a number of longitudinal tracks and dots magnetised across the tape in these tracks. Each character is represented by a unique pattern of dots, often using the same binary code as that used in representing the data in the internal store of the processor. One track may be used for parity checking purposes in the same way as on punched paper tape. Recording densities vary from system to system but can be up to 900 characters to the inch.

C.A.—D*

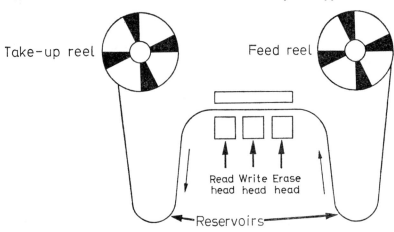

Take-up reel   Feed reel

Read Write Erase
head head head

Reservoirs

Note (i) The erase head may not be required depending on
        the tape system
     (ii) A "dual purpose" head used for reading and
        writing may be fitted

Fig.   7.5—Example of Magnetic Tape Deck Layout (International
                    Computers Ltd.)

Data is organised on the tape in the following way:

First, a number of characters are assembled into what is called a
FIELD. A number of fields together comprise what is called a
RECORD. As a practical example of how these terms are used,
there might be one record for each item of stock in a stock control
system. This record could consist of four fields, one each for part
number, description, quantity and unit price, and each field would
consist of the number of characters necessary to accommodate the
information.

RECORD			
FIELD	FIELD	FIELD	FIELD
Part Number	Description	Quantity	Unit Price
4 characters	15 characters	3 characters	10 characters

As we have seen, data will be read into the internal storage of the central processor when it is required. The amount of data read in each time will depend, to a certain extent, on the amount of internal storage available to receive it, but will in any case, be one or more complete records. The name given to a group of records transferred to the internal storage at any one time is a BLOCK.

A number of characters	=	a Field
A number of fields	=	a Record
A number of records	=	a Block

Having said this it must be emphasised that the number of characters to a field, the number of fields to a record and the number of records to a block need not be constant. In other words magnetic tape can use a variable-field, a variable-record and a variable-block length format for recording data. This in itself gives rise to the problem of distinguishing one field from another, one record from another and one block from another, a problem that does not arise when it is known beforehand that each field, record and block contains a constant number of sub-divisions.

Two of the more commonly used ways of indicating where one item ends and the next begins are the use of special 'markers' inserted at the end of each item or the use of 'counts' inserted at the beginning of each item. A 'marker' consists of a special pattern of magnetised areas indicating the end of a field, a record or a block. Thus we could have End of Field Marker, End of Record Marker and End of Block Marker. A 'count' is made by the central processor counting the number of characters in a field, the number of fields in a record and the number of records in a block and recording these numbers on the tape preceding the data. In this way the computer, when reading, can distinguish between these three units of data.

In order to give the tape time to accelerate to the required speed and to slow down to a stop before and after reading a block, spaces are left on the tape between blocks. These are known as Inter-block Gaps. An illustration of the organisation of data on a tape using markers is given in fig. 7.6 (a) and (b).

Since a large proportion of the time involved in using tape is taken up by starting, accelerating, slowing and stopping, the number of starts and stops is minimised by keeping blocks as large as possible compatable with the size of the computer's store.

In response to a 'read' instruction one block of data is transferred

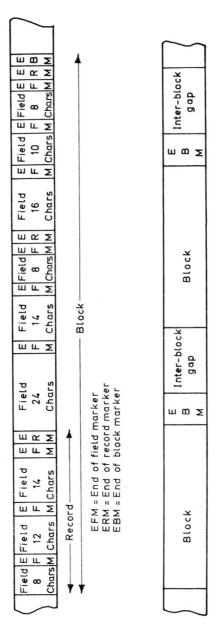

EFM = End of field marker
ERM = End of record marker
EBM = End of block marker

Fig. 7.6 (a)—Organisation of data on Magnetic Tape with Variable Length Fields

Fig. 7.6 (b)—Organisation of data blocks on Magnetic Tape, showing markers to define block lengths with blocks separated by inter-block gaps

to the computer store. The magnetic tape will then remain at rest at the inter-block gap until the next block is called for. This operation is repeated until the whole file is processed.

On a magnetic tape provision is made for indicating the point at which recording may start and, to avoid over-running the end of the tape, where it must finish. This is done by siting markers on the tape known as 'Load Point Marker' and 'End of Tape Marker' respectively. These are light reflective strips mounted on the reverse side of the tape that are detected by the mechanism of the tape deck. It is between these two markers that recording takes place. However, since the transfer unit to and from the central processor is a Block, sufficient space must be left after the End of Tape marker to complete writing a block of data.

In addition to these two markers, two other factors are incorporated into the tape. These are Labels situated at the beginning and the end of the tape. The first of these, at the beginning of the tape occupying the block immediately following the Load Point marker, is usually known as a Header Label and provides the central processor with the means of identifying that the correct tape has been loaded. It usually contains the following information:

(a) A unique set of characters to identify the block as a header label.

(b) An identification of the reel of tape. This is the serial number allocated by the tape library and remains constant throughout the life of the tape irrespective of the data recorded on it.

(c) Identification of the file contained on the tape by name and also, since one file may be contained on a number of tapes the sequence number of the tape within the file. This part of the label may also contain a file generation number should a number of files of the same title exist at various stages of up-dating. This file identification data is checked against the file identification in the program. Should it not conform with this, processing will not be permitted to start and the operator's intervention is called for.

(d) The date on which the tape was written and the retention period. From this the computer is able to calculate the purge date. If this is equal to or less than the current date, over-writing is permitted, otherwise processing will not start and again the operator's intervention is called for.

The second label, occupying the last block on the tape is known as a Trailer Label. This also contains characters to identify it as a trailer label but a most important purpose is to indicate whether the file is now finished or is continued on a further tape, identifying if appropriate the continuation tape. It is usual for one section of the trailer label to record a count of the number of data blocks on the tape, a 'Block Count'. This, at the end of the tape run, is checked against a count made in the central processor of blocks as they are processed, so as to show if any have been missed. Fig. 7.7 illustrates the layout of a magnetic tape with markers and labels.

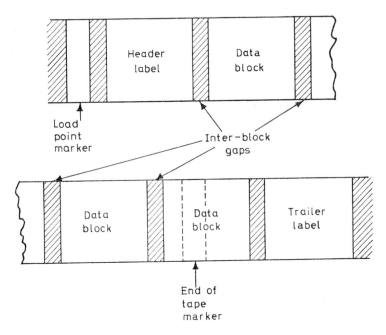

Fig. 7.7—Layout of Magnetic Tape showing Markers and Labels

Example of processing using magnetic tape.

We will consider the example quoted earlier in this chapter of a Sales Ledger System where movement data, Sales, Returns, Cash etc. have to be posted to Sales Ledger Accounts.

Initially a Master Tape would be prepared containing customer name and address, account reference and opening balance. Movement data would then be written to a second tape probably from punched cards prepared from the source documentation.

The two tapes are then linked on-line to the central processor.

Data is read into the store processor from the master tape for the first account and then the movement data relating to the same account from the second tape. The master data and movement data are merged, at the same time calculating a new balance, and then written to a third tape. This third tape now becomes the master tape for the next up-dating run (see fig. 7.8).

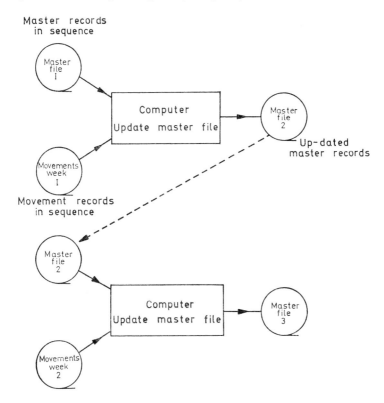

Fig. 7.8—Processing data held on Magnetic Tape—Up-dating runs

RANDOM OR DIRECT ACCESS STORES

One major disadvantage in the backing stores so far considered is that data can only be read from them in the same order as it was recorded. If it is required to select a data item at random a search has to be made through all the items until the required data is found. This is a fairly lengthy business entailing transferring every record to the central processor for scrutiny until the correct one is found.

Random access storage enables the computer to select any item of data irrespective of where it is stored in relation to the other items. The Magnetic Drum is one type of random access store and this has already been discussed earlier in this chapter under the heading Internal Storage. It should be emphasised, however, that when this form of storage is used in modern computers it is as a Backing store.

Other forms of random access store are:

Magnetic Disc Storage

This consists of a number of discs each with two recording surfaces, mounted on a central spindle. Each surface has a number of concentric recording rings known as 'tracks' and each track in turn is divided into a number of Data Sectors separated from each other by inter-sector gaps. Each sector can record a number of characters. Since the innermost concentric rings will have a smaller circumference than those on the outside of the disc, in some disc units, namely Fixed Disc Stores they contain fewer data sectors. The size of a data sector will vary from system to system but, for example, in one system a data sector contains sixty 25-bit words.

Each word is allocated its own individual address by reference to the Disc, the Track and the Data Sector in which it is located. Writing to and reading from the disc is through read/write heads located above and below each disc. These heads are mounted on movable arms enabling any track on any disc to be located.

The discs revolve between the read/write heads so that each data sector passes a head in turn. The time taken to access any data word on any disc is the time for the head carrier arm to move through the distance necessary to locate the correct track and the time for the disc to revolve until the required sector is located under or over the reading head. Average access time is around 135 milliseconds. Fig. 7.9 shows diagramatically a disc surface and Fig. 7.10 a disc assembly with read/write heads.

While disc sizes vary from installation to installation, a disc store will hold a very large volume of data. For example, a store of sixteen 31 inch discs will store in the region of 30,000,000 characters, any one of which can be selected for transfer to the central processor in an average time of about a sixth of a second.

Two types of Disc Store are commonly used.

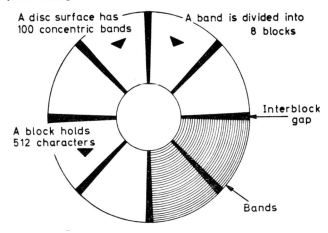

A disc surface holds 102,400 words or 409,600 characters

Fig. 7.9—Illustration of disc surface. (International Computers Ltd.)

Six discs ten recording surfaces

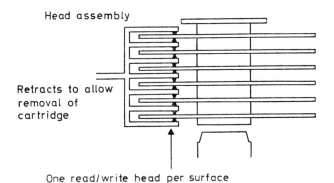

Fig. 7.10—A diagrammatic representation of a disc assembly with
reading heads in position. (International Computers Ltd.)

Fixed Disc Store

As the name implies, in this case the discs remain permanently fixed in the device for on-line computer use. Information is written to and read from the discs as required. If necessary it can be erased and replaced with other data.

Exchangeable Disc Store

In this case, cartridges of discs, usually six in number, are loaded on and off the unit as required. In this way a library of discs can be kept for a variety of applications and used for processing as required. The capacity of Exchangeable Discs is usually not as great as Fixed Discs. A Cartridge of six two-sided discs will contain about 6,000,000 characters.

Magnetic Card Store

This is another form of random access store. Basically it consists of a number of cards having a magnetisable surface on one side. Sizes vary from manufacturer to manufacturer but a typical size is $16'' \times 4\frac{1}{2}''$. Data is recorded on longitudinal tracks across the face of the card, each track being divided into a number of blocks.

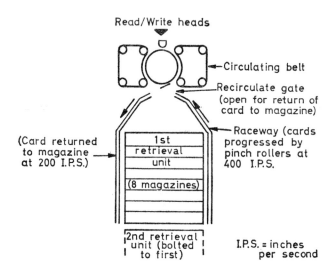

Fig. 7.11—Magnetic Card file unit (plan) (International Computers Ltd.)

Data is located by reference to the card, the track and the block within the track. Cards are stored in magazines containing about 200 cards. Recording capacity is in the region of 160,000 characters a card giving a total magazine capacity of some 32,000,000 characters. A number of magazines can be stored in the machine at the same time.

Read/write operations are carried out by selecting an individual card from the appropriate magazine and passing it over a series of rollers until it reaches a read/write head. Speed of transference to the head can be about 200 inches per second. As the card passes over the head data is written to or read from the required location and it then passes back, through another series of rollers to its original place in the magazine. (See Fig. 7.11.) Access time again will vary from system to system but is usually somewhere between 150 and 400 milli-seconds.

For selection purposes each card has a unique pattern of indentations along one edge to identify it. Selection is made by reference to this pattern.

EXERCISES CHAPTER 7

1. Compare and contrast magnetic tape and magnetic disc files and indicate the most appropriate methods of arranging files on these media to gain efficient processing.
   (Institute of Data Processing.)
2. What do you understand by the terms:
   (a) Master data.
   (b) Movement data.
   (c) Updating.
   Use any system of your choice to illustrate your answer.
3. Compare and contrast exchangeable disc packs and magnetic tape as methods of providing backing store with modern computer configurations.
   (Institute of Data Processing.)
4. Define and illustrate the difference between random and serial access stores.
   (Royal Society of Arts—Computer Appreciation—Stage I)
5. What is a Backing store?
   List the types of backing stores available and explain how these work in relation to the central processor store.

6. What are the disadvantages of:
   (a) Punched cards or
   (b) Punched paper tape when used for storing large volumes of data.
7. Explain how data is recorded on magnetic tape, and how data items may be located.
8. Draw a diagram to show how data is recorded on magnetic tape. What is the difference between fixed and variable length fields? Give examples of the use of each.
9. What do you understand by the term 'up-dating'. Draw a diagram to show how a Master Stock Ledger File would be up-dated by issues and receipts from store.
10. Compare and contrast a Fixed Disc store with an Exchangeable Disc store.
11. Explain what is meant by the following terms:
    (a) A block—in relation to Magnetic Tape.
    (b) A Field.
    (c) A Record.
12. Explain how data is recorded on a magnetic drum and how data items may be located.
13. Describe in detail the format of records on Magnetic Tape. Explain what is meant by:
    (a) Label
    (b) Inter-block Gap
    (c) Packing Density
    (d) Beginning of Tape Marker.
    (Royal Society of Arts—Computer Appreciation Stage II)
14. Random access files are often claimed to be superior to magnetic tape files, which are sequential. What do the terms 'Random access' and 'Sequential' mean in this context?
15. What equipments are now available to permit direct access to information in a computer system? Which of these in your view provides the greatest advantages in operation (give reasons)
    (Institute of Data Processing.)
16. Draw a block diagram for a typical computer configuration, for the handling of bulk data at high speed.
    Describe in outline the applications of:
    (a) drum storage
    (b) magnetic tape storage
    (Royal Society of Arts—Computer Appreciation—Stage I).

8

Flowcharts and Decision Tables

Flowcharting is a convenient way of expressing on paper in diagrammatic form the activities involved in attaining a required
objective, and the sequence in which these activities must be performed. As a recording technique it serves three useful purposes.
As an aid to working out how a problem can best be solved, as a
means of illustrating a proposed system for management consideration and as a permanent record of procedures and activities, to be
used as a standard for operating purposes.

FLOWCHARTS

PREPARING FLOWCHARTS
The basic factors with which we are concerned when constructing
a flowchart are:

(a) An Objective
In other words we start with an aim in mind—the flowchart is
the process of working out how this aim can be achieved.

(b) A Starting Point
This is some circumstance or event that triggers off the series of
activities necessary to achieve the aim. For example, if the aim is to
dig the garden the starting point might just be 'arrive home', or
if to supply a customer with goods 'receive order'.

(c) The Activities that are necessary and the Sequence in which these
must be performed
Now if the circumstances of a situation were always constant
then the activities resulting would always be the same and it would
just be a case of putting them into a logical sequence, a to b, b to c,

c to d and so on. However this is rarely the case. Circumstances tend to vary within a situation giving rise to the need for alternative activities, thus instead of progressing from (a) to (b) we find that (a) will lead to (b) or (c) depending on the circumstances. In flow-charting we are concerned with taking into account all of the circumstances that could arise and defining all of the activities that these give rise to.

(*d*) *Decisions*

This is the process of deciding which alternative activities must be performed in order to reach our aim when faced with differing circumstances. For example, if our starting point is 'receive order from customer', then we are faced with the position that the order may have been received from a Cash customer or from a Credit customer. The aim is the same in each case, the execution of the order, but the activities leading up to this could well be different.

As a simple example to illustrate these four points let us take as an aim 'make a cup to tea'. The starting point might be 'get out of bed', and the activities include 'dress', 'go down stairs', 'fill kettle', 'put kettle on gas', 'get milk, sugar and tea' etc. This is all very well but what happens if there is no tea? In other words we are faced with one of two situations 'there is some tea' or 'there is no tea'. In the first case the next activity might be 'put tea in teapot' and in the second case 'go next door and borrow some tea'. If we trace this second series of activities the next thing to ask is 'get any tea from next door?', if the answer is yes we can go back to the first series and 'put tea in teapot', if it is no, then we must consider what further activities are necessary to achieve our aim.

With these four factors in mind, the following is suggested as an approach to the construction of a flowchart:

(a)   Make a note of the aim of the chart.

(b)   Decide at what point the series of activities are going to start.

(c)   Make a note of the main activities that are likely to be involved trying to put them in a logical order, although the best order may not become apparent until the chart is under way.

(d)   Start with the first activity and decide what different actions this could give rise to.

(e)   One at a time, trace these actions arising out of a decision, going as far as possible with one before going back to the alternatives.

(f)   Show each action once only on the flowchart, using flowlines and connectors to go back to it whenever necessary.

The flowchart will be constructed by the use of symbols connected with flow lines with arrows indicating the direction of flow. The activities should be briefly described either in the symbols themselves or as notes appended to the flowchart and cross referenced to the symbols. A Flowchart Symbols Template should be used for drawing the symbols, and the connecting lines should be straight, either vertical or horizontal. While there are recognised methods of drawing flowcharts horizontally, that is starting at the left and proceeding to the right-hand side of the paper, it is more usual in systems and program flowcharting to construct them vertically, from top to bottom of the paper. Attention should be paid to the layout of the chart in the sense that it should be well balanced, symbol sizes should be consistent within the one chart and evenly spaced as far as possible. It is important that final flowcharts should be neat, with legible writing so that no difficulty in interpretation will arise when it is used by people other than the compiler.

The four most commonly used symbols in flowcharting are illustrated below, but for charting systems and programs a wide range of symbols are available. These are shown in fig. 8.2., pp. 113-118.

Used for any form of action. The action is usually described in the box.

Decision Box. Used to lead to different actions.

Terminal Box. Showing the start or finish of a procedure.

Connecting Box. Connects one section of a flowchart with another.

An illustration of a simple flowchart using these four symbols is given in fig. 8.1.

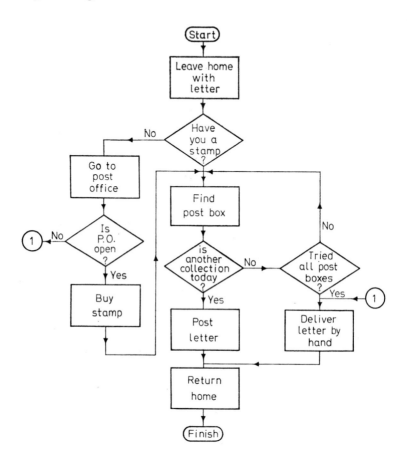

Fig. 8.1—Flowchart illustrating the use of four basic symbols

Fig 8.2: SYMBOLS USED IN PROGRAM
FLOW CHARTS

GENERAL OPERATIONAL SYMBOL.
Representing any kind of processing
function, or used for any operation for
which no particular symbol has been
defined.

PRE-DEFINED PROCESS SYMBOL.
Representing a named process consisting
of one or more operations or program
steps. e.g. a program segment or a sub-
routine.

INPUT/OUTPUT. Indicating making
available information for processing, or
recording processed information.

PREPARATION SYMBOL. Represents
the modification of an instruction or
group of instructions which change the
program itself. e.g. Initialise a routine,
set a Switch, or modify an Index Register.

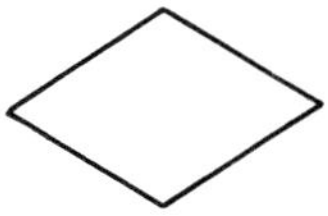

BRANCH SYMBOL. Has one entry line
and more than one exit line. Represents a
decision that determines the exit path to
be taken.

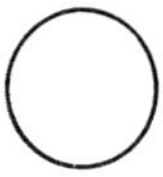

CONNECTOR. Represents exit to or
entry from another point in the program.
Must contain a reference to relate exit
and entry points.

Fig 8.2 (*cont.*)

TERMINAL. Used for the beginning or end of a flow line e.g. start, stop, halt, interrupt, delay.

COMMENT SYMBOL. To add additional information, explanations etc.

FLOW LINES.
These connect successive program steps. Lines should be straight, left to right or top to bottom.

Arrows are used to specify direction of flow when necessary.

Flow lines crossing, having no logical inter-relation.

Flow line junction.

Fig 8.2 (*cont.*)

In addition to the above symbols, the following are used in Systems Flow Charts.

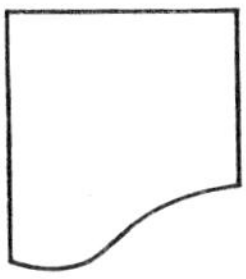

DOCUMENT. Used to represent a document input to or output from a system or computer.

PUNCHED CARD. Representing the use of Punched Cards in a system.

DECK OF PUNCHED CARDS.

PUNCHED PAPER TAPE.

MAGNETIC TAPE. Representing magnetic tape input or output.

MAGNETIC DRUM. Representing magnetic drum storage.

Fig 8.2 (*cont.*)

MAGNETIC DISC. Used to represent either fixed or exchangeable disc stores.

CORE SYMBOL. Representing internal Central Processor storage.

VISUAL DISPLAY. Representing the use of a visual display unit in conjunction with a computer.

GRAPH PLOTTER. Representing use of graph plotter with a computer.

MERGING SYMBOL. Represents combining two or more sets of items in sequence according to a common key, into one set of items.

EXTRACT SYMBOL. To represent an operation which removes one or more sets of items from a single set.

Fig 8.2 (*cont.*)

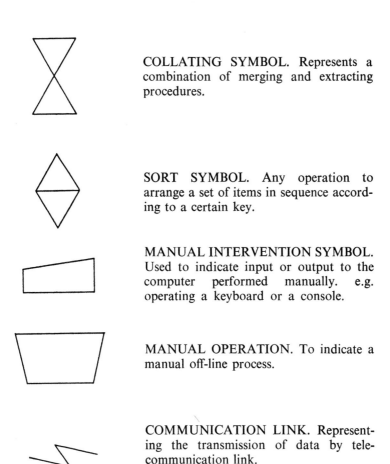

COLLATING SYMBOL. Represents a combination of merging and extracting procedures.

SORT SYMBOL. Any operation to arrange a set of items in sequence according to a certain key.

MANUAL INTERVENTION SYMBOL. Used to indicate input or output to the computer performed manually. e.g. operating a keyboard or a console.

MANUAL OPERATION. To indicate a manual off-line process.

COMMUNICATION LINK. Representing the transmission of data by telecommunication link.

Fig 8.2 (*cont.*)

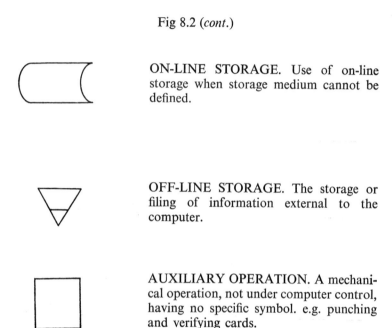

ON-LINE STORAGE. Use of on-line storage when storage medium cannot be defined.

OFF-LINE STORAGE. The storage or filing of information external to the computer.

AUXILIARY OPERATION. A mechanical operation, not under computer control, having no specific symbol. e.g. punching and verifying cards.

So far we have used the term Flowchart in a general sense as a chart showing a sequence of activities. In computer work different forms of chart are used at different stages in the development and definition of a system, showing different degrees of detail. While there appears to be no generally accepted terminology for these, they can be classified as follows:
1. Block Charts. Showing in broad outline the sequence of activities in a system.

2. Systems Flow Charts. Showing the sequence of activities and procedures in more detail.
3. Program Flow Charts. These are concerned with those parts of the system that are computer processed and show the operations, in sequence, that the computer will perform.

BLOCK CHART

Perhaps this could be called the simplest form of Flowchart. It shows the sequence of the main procedures within a system without showing in detail how these are carried out. It is usual to use only one symbol, a rectangle, to indicate each procedure and into this is written a short narrative explanation. These rectangles are joined by flow lines to indicate direction of flow. The chart is often supported by more detailed notes, the notes being cross-referenced to the number contained in the rectangle. An example of a section of a block chart is shown in fig. 8.3. This shows the main procedures in a routine for dealing with orders received from credit customers.

SYSTEMS FLOWCHART

This expands the Block Chart, breaking each procedure down into more detailed operations and again showing the sequence in which these operations are performed. It is constructed using standard flowchart symbols. As with a blockchart it should be accompanied by a narrative description either written into the boxes or appended separately and referenced to the boxes.

Unlike the blockchart where it is usually possible to show a whole routine in broad outline in one chart, the additional detail in a systems flowchart often makes this impractical, and a series of charts are made for different sections of the routine. These are inter-related by the use of connector symbols. In contrast to a program flowchart, a systems flowchart does not just specify the procedures that are computer processed, but is concerned with the system as a whole. The flowchart can often be conveniently sectionalised. For example, one section may deal with the manual procedures up to the time source documents are received by the computer department, another with the procedures involved in the data preparation stage, a third for the computer processing operations and a fourth showing the routine for dealing with output reports. Fig. 8.4 illustrates a systems flowchart, showing the procedures for dealing with orders up to the time the documents are passed to the computer department for processing. Further examples of flowcharts will be found in chapter 13 dealing with Applications.

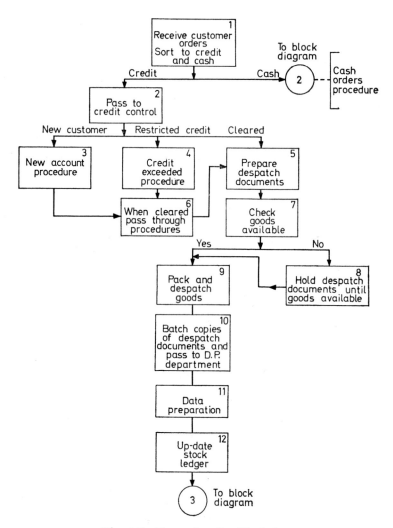

Fig. 8.3—Example of a Blockchart

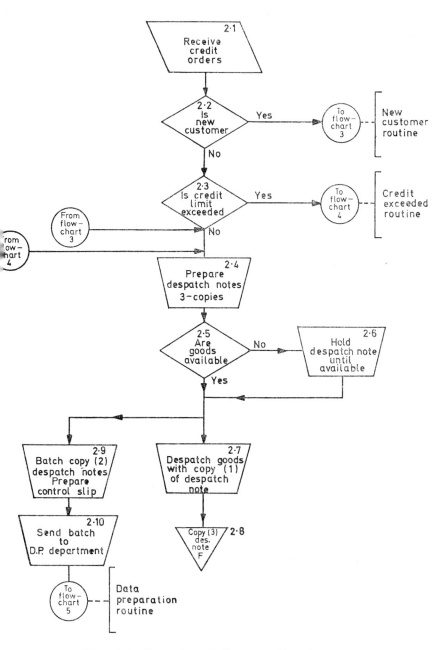

Fig. 8.4—Example of Systems Flowchart

PROGRAM FLOWCHART

From the systems flowchart we now move to a more detailed definition of that part of the system to be computer processed, that is a Program Flowchart specifying the computer operations. Since it is from this that the list of instructions making up the computer program will be encoded, it will be appreciated that a program flowchart must be constructed in a very detailed form. However, with a lengthy and complex system, it is not always possible to convert the systems flowchart to a program flowchart giving the required amount of detail, in one stage. For this reason program flowcharts are often constructed at a series of 'levels' each succeeding level expanding into greater detail the information contained in the chart at the previous level. The terms Outline Program Flowchart and Detailed Program Flowchart are often used in this context. The outline chart records the main run of the program, showing the various procedures involved, and then detailed charts constructed for each of the procedures showing in detail the operations necessary to accomplish the procedure. These outline procedures shown in the first chart are usually known as program Segments.

Fig. 8.5 illustrates a simple outline program flowchart for updating a Stock Ledger. This contains two segments, 'A' and 'B', the latter being the subject of the detailed program flowchart, shown in fig. 8.6.

Finally, one or two general points. Constructing flowcharts is to a great extent a matter of trial and error. It is initially a process of experimentation involving repeated attempts and modifications until a final solution is reached. Having completed a flowchart it must not be taken as necessarily the best, or even a correct solution. It must be thoroughly checked for both the accuracy of its logic and for its adequacy to deal with all of the possible variations of the problem it is intended to solve. Probably the best way of doing this is to trace the course of test input data through it, thus simulating the actual computer operations. Care should be taken however, to ensure that sufficient variations of input data are tested so as to be representative of all of the situations catered for in the program.

It should be borne in mind that different people will be involved at different stages in the preparation of flowcharts. It is, therefore, important that the chart should be clear, not only to the person constructing it but to others who will work from it. A good flowchart has clear writing, a neat presentation and uses agreed symbols.

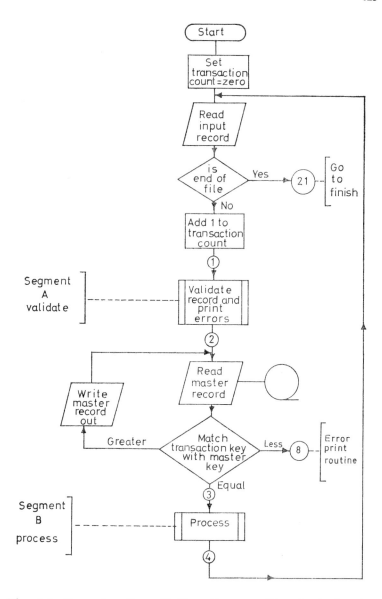

Fig. 8.5—Example of an Outline Program Flowchart showing
Program Segments

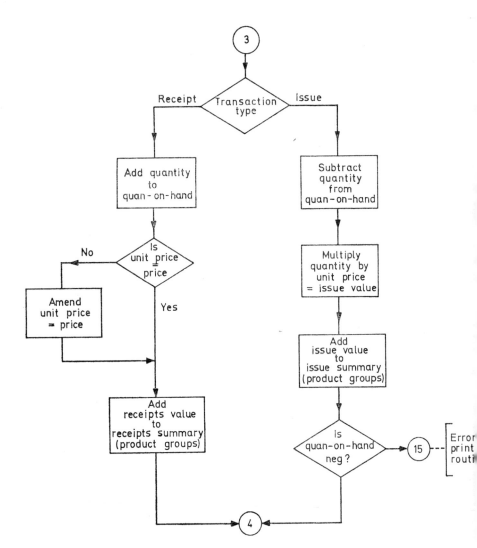

Fig. 8.6—Detailed Program Flowchart for Segment 'B' fig. 8.5

DECISION TABLES

In the analysis and design of computer systems it is often difficult to appreciate all of the aspects of a problem and all of the possible situations that might arise from a set of circumstances. The purpose of a decision table is to set out in a formal way all of the factors that need to be considered and the procedure that any combination of these factors will give rise to. The factors taken into consideration are called Conditions, the different combinations of these factors are known as Condition Rules and the procedure the condition rules give rise to are known as Action Rules.

For example, when servicing a car we might say 'If the petrol is low and if the oil is low I will get some petrol and some oil'. Now within this situation there are two conditions, Is the Petrol low? and is the Oil low? This in turn leads us to four different combinations of conditions, or Condition Rules. Both petrol and oil are low, only petrol is low, only oil is low and neither are low. The four alternative courses of action, or Action Rules, arising from these condition rules are—get petrol and oil, get petrol, get oil and get neither. This problem is set out in the form of a decision table in fig. 8.7.

Decision table

Conditions	Rule number			
	1	2	3	4
Is petrol low ?	Y	Y	N	N
Is oil low ?	Y	N	Y	N
Actions	Action rules			
Get petrol	X	X		
Get oil	X		X	
Get neither				X

Fig. 8.7—Example of a simple Decision Table

The top half of the table contains a list of conditions on the left hand side with a number of vertical columns on the right headed Rule Number. These contain the different combinations of conditions. If the condition is present it is indicated by inserting a 'Y' for Yes, otherwise an 'N' for No. The lower half of the table lists the possible actions that could arise, showing those resulting from any given combination of conditions by inserting 'X's' in the appropriate columns.

In order to ensure that every possible combination of conditions is taken into account, the number of condition rules can be determined as being equal to 2^n where n is the number of conditions. Having found the possible number of combinations, to ensure that each combination is unique the following rule, known as the Halve Rule is applied.

In the first row Y's are repeated for one half of the number of condition rules, that is 2^{n-1} times, followed by the same number of N's. In the second row, groups of Y's and N's alternate, the size of the groups being one half of those in the first row. This means Y's and N's are repeated 2^{n-2} times. This process of halving the group size is repeated for successive rows until the final row contains single Y's and N's. Fig. 8.8 illustrates this process in a table containing three conditions. In this case n being equal to three, the number of condition rules is 2^3 equals 8. The first row contains a block of Y's equal to one half of this number, i.e. four, followed by a similar block of N's. The second row blocks of Y's and N's one half the size of those in the first row, the size of these blocks being in turn halved for the third row.

To simplify the table by reducing the number of condition rules, if two rules, different in one row only, result in the same action, then these two rules can be combined. This is done by placing a dash '—' in the appropriate row. An example of this is shown in fig. 8.9 where rules 1 and 2, the same except for row three, result in the same action. That is, the performance of condition three is immaterial to the action taken. The same situation occurs in rules 7 and 8. By combining these two pairs of rules the number of rules is reduced to six. This principle is known as the Dash Rule.

This now means that the number of rules is no longer equal to 2^n.

In order to prove that all rules have been considered a Dash Count column is added to the right of the condition rules in which the number of rules absorbed is entered. This dash count plus the number of rules will now reconcile with 2^n.

When considering the combinations of conditions in a decision

Decision table

Table number 146	Table name: Course entry	Date 30th Sept.	Author B.Smith														
		Rule number															
	Conditions	1	2	3	4	5	6	7	8	9	10	11	12	13	14	15	16
C1	3 G.C.E passes	Y	Y	Y	Y	N	N	N	N								
C2	Good school report	Y	Y	N	N	Y	Y	N	N								
C3	Satisfactory interview	Y	N	Y	N	Y	N	Y	N								
	Actions.																
A1	Accept applicant	X	X	X		X											
A2	Reject applicant				X		X	X	X								

Fig. 8.8—A Decision Table showing rules for admission to college of applicants who must satisfy two of the three conditions

DECISION TABLE

Table number 146	Table name. Course entry	Date 30th Sept	Author B.Smith		Rule number.																D/C
				1	2	3	4	5	6	7	8	9	10	11	12	13	14	15	16	
	Conditions																			
C1	3 GCE passes			Y	Y	Y	N	N	N											
C2	Good school report			Y	N	N	Y	Y	N											
C3	Satisfactory interview			—	Y	N	Y	N	—											2
	Actions																			
A1	Accept applicant			X	X		X													
A2	Reject applicant					X		X	X											

Fig. 8.9—Decision Table showing the application of the 'Dash Rule'

table it is sometimes found that some rules represent either an impossible situation or that the occurrence is highly unlikely. In order to save specifying these rules use may be made of what is known as the Else Rule. This requires the insertion of the word 'else' after the entry of all the rules from which anticipated action will result. This means it denotes an exceptional or unanticipated condition that requires special treatment. However this rule should be used with great care as it introduces the possibility of a relevant set of conditions being missed.

Advantages claimed for the decision table method over other forms of charting are:

(a) The problem is more easily defined. It helps to identify the problem and the rules associated with it.
(b) Provides an element of control over analysis and design. That is it positively determines the number of different conditions and the action arising from each.
(c) It provides a uniform method of describing the logic of a system.
(d) It is a means of communicating the logic of a situation to programmers.
(e) Since the logic can be broken down into small natural modules it facilitates the amendment of a system. It eases the problem of keeping a system up to date with changing conditions.

Finally it is not suggested that decision tables can take the place of flowcharts, but rather that they supplement these by ensuring that all circumstances are taken into consideration.

EXERCISES CHAPTER 8

1. Draw a flowchart to illustrate the activities involved in borrowing a specific book from a library.
2. On 10 separate occasions an observer records the numbers of men, women and children using an escalator. Each set of observations is punched into a card or to paper tape in this order:
   (a) Men
   (b) Women
   (c) Children.
   Draw a flow diagram to read in this data, process it and provide the following output:
   (a) The separate totals of men, women and children.
   (b) The average number of children per observation.
   (Royal Society of Arts—Computer Appreciation—Stage I)

3. A Credit Control Department rates customer accounts as A, B or C. When accounts are 30 days overdue a reminder is sent to B and C accounts if the amount outstanding is more than £10, and to A accounts if the amount is more than £25. For amounts of £10 or less no action is taken until the accounts are 60 days overdue when a reminder is sent to all customers concerned. For B and C accounts, if more than £10 is still outstanding after 60 days a warning is sent to the customer and also, in the case of C accounts a 'Stop Supply' notice is sent to the Sales Office. Accounts rated A are sent a reminder when 60 days overdue if the amount is £25 or less otherwise a warning is sent.
Show the above procedure in flowchart form.
(Institute of Data Processing)

4. Draw a flowchart to read 1,000 cards each containing a number. The numbers are to be added and the result printed.

5. ABC Co. allow discounts when invoicing customers with goods. A bulk order discount of 5 per cent is given on *all* orders in excess of £100. Trade customers receive a trade discount of 10 per cent irrespective of the value of the order, and trade customers who are also members of the ABC Product Group qualify for an additional 5 per cent discount.
Construct a decision table showing the actions to be taken in respect of each type of customer.

6. Draw a flowchart to read 100 cards each containing a positive number and to print out the highest.

7, Draw a flowchart illustrating the activities involved in making a telephone call from a public call box.

8. Passes in an examination at the end of a course are assessed on the following factors:
1.   45 per cent or more marks must be gained in each paper.
2.   An average of 50 per cent marks must be obtained over all papers.
3.   There must be an attendance record of at least 60 per cent at lectures.
4.   Assessment of in-course work must be at least 60 per cent.
A pass is automatically given if all four of the above conditions are met. In the event of the in-course assessment being less than 60 per cent the case is submitted to a moderator for decision providing the other three conditions are met. If the average examination mark is 50 per cent or more but the mark in any of the individual papers is less than 45 per cent, the candidate

is referred in these subjects providing the last two conditions are met. In all other cases the candidate is failed.

(a) Draw up a decision table

(b) Construct a flowchart to illustrate these procedures.

9. A Stores Control Clerk performs the following routine in respect of each requisition for materials issued from store.

(a) Checks Job number on requisition against current Job number list. If not on the list the requisition is referred back for correction.

(b) Looks up the appropriate Stock Record Sheet for each item on the requisition and deducts the requisitioned quantity from the stock balance.

(c) Compares revised stock balance with the re-order level stated on the stock control sheet. If the stock balance is lower he prepares a re-order request after he has checked the physical stock to ensure that this conforms with the amount on the record sheet.

(d) If the physical stock does not agree with the balance on the record sheet he prepares a Stores Discrepancy Note and hands this to the chief Store-keeper. If the physical stock is less than the re-order level he still prepares a re-order request.

Show the above procedure in flowchart form.

10. Draw a block chart that shows the procedures involved in dealing with Purchase Invoices that have to be:

(a) Sorted into Net and Cash Discount settlement terms, and the latter given priority in clearance for payment.

(b) Checked to ensure that the goods charged have been received.

(c) Checked for prices, extensions, calculations and discounts. In the event of error the invoice is referred back to the supplier.

(d) Authorised for payment by the chief buyer.

(e) Remittance Advice prepared.

(f) Cheque drawn.

(g) e and f posted to the supplier.

11. Each card of a deck is punched with a separate record. Draw two flow charts that will cause the contents of each card to be read into the core store of the computer subject to the following conditions.

Flowchart I—where the number of cards is known to be 500.

Flowchart II—where the number of cards is unknown.

Explain the peculiarities of each method by reference to your flowcharts.

Assume that a card may be read by the use of one instruction.

(Royal Society of Arts—Computer Appreciation—Stage I)

12. Consider the following statement:

'Service will be provided on model A once a year during the first two years of use and subsequently twice a year until five years of use have elapsed. Thereafter frequency of service will become the subject of special agreement.

The service agreement for model B is identical except that twice yearly service will be provided during the first two years of use'.

(a) Derive a decision table to satisfy these conditions.

(b) Draw a conventional flowchart to illustrate the same logic.

(c) Indicate briefly what advantage is to be gained by the use of decision tables in expressing logical requirements.

(Institute of Data Processing)

9

Collection, Preparation and Control of Data

It could be said that data is the raw material of a data processing system. It consists of facts and figures which record in detail the many and varied activities of a business. A data item on its own, however, means little unless it is related to other items of data and interpreted within the context of the system as a whole. The aim of data processing is to relate and interpret data records to provide meaningful information in the form of output reports. One data record that B. Brown worked $40\frac{1}{2}$ hours in one week is of little use in itself while again a second data record that B. Brown is paid 60 p an hour is similarly of little use. However, by relating these two records we can produce a report to the effect that the gross pay earned by B. Brown in that particular week was £24·30. If a further record is available that B. Brown spent the $40\frac{1}{2}$ hours making 6 tables, we can begin to interpret these items of data in terms of specific productive activities and production costs.

In data processing we are usually concerned with data of two basic kinds. On the one hand there is data which, while it records information relating to some business activity, remains unchanged for a long period of time. This is known as Master Data, and examples are a Customer's name, address and account number. On the other hand there is data that records the periodic changes in values and quantities related to a business activity, such as the sale of goods to a customer or the receipt of cash. This is known as Movement data.

However, there exists between these two types of data, Master and Movement, an area of data recording that we can call 'up-dated' data, comprising records of current balances and values reflecting the present situation in an organisation. These up-dated balances are amended from time to time by the application of movement data. In the above example then, we are concerned with three factors, Master information—Customer's name, address and reference number, Movement information—transactions between the customer and ourselves and Up-dated information—reflecting the current position which in this case is the balance on the customer account. Master data remains relatively unchanged, Up-dated data reflects the current position, which is kept up to date by the application of Movement data.

A collection of data items relating to a particular procedure is known as a Data File. A Master file contains master and up-dated information and a Movement file contains the data to be applied to the master file for up-dating purposes. The form these files take in an electronic data processing organisation will, of course, depend upon the input and output mechanisms of the computer in use, but master files are usually kept on Magnetic Tape, Magnetic Discs or Magnetic Cards while movement files are created initially on Punched Cards or Punched Paper Tape and either used directly in this form or first transferred to a Magnetic Tape, Card or Disc store and then applied.

Data, whether movement or master, has to be obtained initially from one source or another. Recording master data is a 'once only' operation, carried out when the system is first converted from manual methods and subject to only occasional amendment, for example, to add a new customer or to alter an address. Up-dated data is, of course, a product of the system arising out of the interaction of master and movement data.

Recording movement data, since this represents a minute by minute record of the activities of a business, is a continuous process. It is the purpose of the next section of this chapter to discuss the organisation of movement data and the processes through which it must pass so that the required results will be produced. To make a list of these processes that would apply to all forms of movement data and to all systems involving movement data would be impractical, in view of the variations in techniques used for the origination of data and the variety of machines used in its processing. However, the types of factor that will determine procedure are:

(a) How is the data recorded at source? Does it originate in machine-readable form such as M.I.C.R. or O.C.R., in a form that can be automatically converted such as Mark Sensing or does it need manual conversion into Punched Cards or Paper Tape?

(b) What kind of machine input is used? Is the input form used direct for processing or first converted to another form, say Magnetic Tape?

(c) What storage devices are available? Are these serial or random access? This factor, together with (b) could well determine what sorting and merging operations must be performed on the data records.

(d) In what form is the output required?

Bearing in mind these factors, which will have an obvious influence on the way in which movement data is processed, the following operations, some or all of which may be applied to data in specific circumstances, will be considered:

1. The initial recording of data at source.
2. Conversion of data to a machine acceptable and machine readable form.
3. Sorting and assembling data into a required sequence.
4. Control of data flow and data content.
5. Control of data accuracy.

DATA ORIGINATION

Data records specify in detail the many and varied activities of a business and could well originate at a number of different sources. We might have Stock Inventory movement data from a Stores office, Cash receipts from an Accounts office, records of hours worked from a Works office. Not only will the data come from different sources but they will be in a number of different forms. Some may be hand-written, some prepared by machine, some containing records in both forms. The name we use for the medium on which this original data is recorded is a Source Document. These source documents will be created not only in the organisation itself but some will flow into the system from outside—supplier's invoices, customer's orders and so on.

While some source documents are prepared from the start in a machine usable form, (e.g. M.I.C.R. or O.C.R. documents) most source documents have to be converted to Punched Card or Paper Tape for machine input purposes.

It is essential that source documents should be prepared in a way which:

(a) Presents data in the most convenient way for conversion, and

(b) Minimises the need to refer back to the source department for checking.

To these ends the order in which data appears on the document, its legibility and accuracy, and the punctual despatch of documents to the Data Processing department are all very important.

Whether the input form is Punched Card or Paper Tape, the order in which the data fields are to be punched must be rigidly defined and also, where applicable, the maximum size of fields. To simplify punching, the data on the source document should be arranged in the same order as that in which fields are keyed in. Where possible the limitations in field size should also be indicated on the source document. Many data records contain non-variable information (such as a transaction code) which could well be pre-printed on the source document. A way of preparing source documents to conform with these principles is suggested in figure 9.1.

In a manual system, documents recording data usually pass through a number of hands, each person performing a given operation until the process is complete. A Stores Requisition, for example, might have the quantities and descriptions entered by one person, the unit price entered by a second, the calculations (unit price multiplied by quantity), performed by a third, the entry into a Stores Issues Summary by a fourth and the posting into a costing system by a fifth person. By and large, the more people there are dealing with a document the greater is the chance of any inaccuracies being detected somewhere along the chain. In an Electronic Data Processing system, once the source document has been prepared, there will probably be only one more reference to the data and that is at the punching stage. From this point onwards only automatic processes will be involved, so the opportunities for people to notice errors are much more limited. This emphasises the need for a very high degree of accuracy in preparing the source documents. Techniques for applying machine checks on accuracy are considered later in this chapter.

The conversion of the source document to a machine input form involves an operator in reading the document, possibly encoding the data, and then entering it into a keyboard. Illegible writing will result either in time being wasted while the document is checked back to source, or in inaccurate data being transcribed. The data processing department must insist on a high degree of accuracy and legibility when source documents are prepared.

Given a satisfactory level of accuracy and legibility, there is still a possibility of error arising from a complete source document going astray or indeed from a punched card being lost. This makes it very necessary to impose some form of control over the flow of the documents. This is discussed in the chapter on Organisation, but briefly, the most efficient way of doing this is to serially number all source documents and to forward them to the processing department in batches arranged in sequence, quoting on the slip

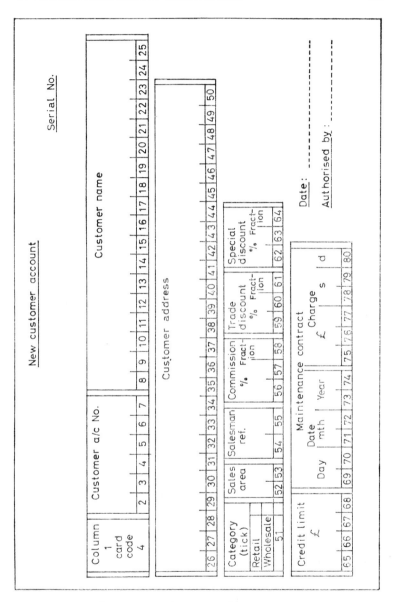

Fig. 9.1—Specimen Punching Document

accompanying the batch the highest and lowest numbers in the sequence. The batches themselves should also be numbered in sequence and the batch number quoted.

The Control section of the D.P. Department can then check that the sequence is complete, making a note of the batch and serial number in a register. This method should reveal the absence of any individual document and also show if a complete batch has gone astray.

A further consideration in the preparation of source documentation is punctuality. A D.P. department works to a fairly rigid time schedule and it is important that source data should be received in time for the conversion process to take place, checks to be made and the data assembled for the machine room by the time the machine run is due to take place. User departments must be informed of deadlines for the receipt of source documents. Finally, source documents should be accompanied with an authority for their acceptance into the data processing system. This may, in the case of routine documents, be the initials of the originating authority on the control slip, but for more important documents, such as requests to draw cheques, each separate document should be initialled.

DATA CONVERSION

As has already been indicated, source documents will usually require conversion to a machine input form, usually punched card or punched paper tape. The mechanics of punching are discussed in detail in the chapter on Input Devices. As in the preparation of source documents, stress must be laid on the need to preserve complete accuracy and to control the flow of data through the punching process. It should be possible to ensure accuracy by a verification process, bearing in mind that the corrected errors must themselves be verified to ensure the accuracy of the correction. Safeguards must also be imposed to prevent cards going astray after punching and verification. In a data preparation section dealing with very large volumes of data the possibility of whole batches of cards being mislaid cannot be ignored. Rigid adherence to a batch system with efficient written control of the progress of batches through the section, and the comparison of totals after punching with those obtained previously from the source documents, should not only reveal the absence of any individual cards or batches but also give an additional check on punching accuracy.

SORTING AND MERGING DATA

Source data, by nature of the activities that give rise to it, is usually generated in random order. For example, it is highly unlikely that issues of stock items from a factory or warehouse store will be in stock item number sequence. However, the master data for a Stock Inventory system will probably be kept on file in item number sequence. We then have the problem of 'marrying-up' movement data in random order with master data in sequence. It would be as well to make a note at this point that the extent of this problem will depend on the type of file used and the way in which data is organised in it. If direct access files are used with records stored either in sequential or random order then direct posting of movement records in random order presents no major difficulty.

It is, however, more often than not, that master records are held in sequence on magnetic tape, the sequence being governed by a 'key' that is part of the data record. This key is a means of identifying the record. In a Stock Inventory system it would probably be the Stock Item Number, in a Sales Ledger system the Customer Account Number. In order to save confusion, a unique range of numbers is usually allocated to each function, for example, Stock Item Numbers 1,000–1,999, Sales Ledger Accounts 2,000–2,999. This key is quoted in every data record so as to identify it with the particular stock item, ledger account etc., to which it refers. In order to process movement data against a master file with records in sequence in this form, it is first necessary to sort the movement data into the same order as the sequence of the records on the master file. There are two approaches to this problem.

1. To sort the data after its conversion but before processing.
2. To write the data on to magnetic tape in random order and then use the computer to sort the data items into sequence on the tape.

Sorting before processing

This method is only practical with input forms that contain one record only per document i.e., unit record systems. This excludes Punched Paper Tape on which, because it is a continuous strip of paper, the items cannot be re-arranged, and also excludes punched cards with more than one data record on one card. For example, a card recording a sales order could contain the Customer Account number and Customer Order number recorded once only at the beginning of the record, followed by a succession of Stock Reference numbers and quantities representing the list of goods ordered. Now while a batch of these cards can be sorted into customer account number order for up-dating a Sales Ledger, the Stock Reference numbers cannot be sorted into sequence for Stock Control up-dating.

Input forms then that can be pre-sorted for processing are Punched Cards, unless they are prepared in the format described above, M.I.C.R. documents and O.C.R. documents. While the mechanics of reading these documents is different in each case (as has been described in chapter 4), the basic method of sorting is much the same. As a result, although punched card sorting is described below, the principles can be applied to the sorting of other machine-readable documents.

A machine known as a Punched Card Sorter is used, which consists of a magazine into which the cards are fed and a sensing device to locate the whereabouts of the holes in a selected column. There are a number of stackers to receive the cards as they pass through the machine, one for each of the twelve punching positions, and one to receive the cards that are rejected. The key, Account Number, Stock Item Number etc., on which the cards are sorted will usually occupy a number of columns and the cards will have to be passed through the machine several times to sort them into the required sequence. There is a device for selecting the column on which the sort is to be made for each pass through the machine.

For example, the following is the routine for sorting cards into numerical order from a four figure key number punched into columns 6 to 9. First the selecting device is set at column 9, the cards are put into the magazine and passed through the machine. All cards with the key number ending in '0' will be deposited in the '0' stacker, the '1's' into the '1' stacker and so on up to 9. The cards are now removed from the stackers, the 0 cards first, the 1 cards placed on top of these and so on until they have all been extracted. The selecting device is now set at the next column to the left, column 8, representing the 10's position in the key number and passed a second time through the machine in the same order as they were extracted after the first pass. The cards will be deposited in the stacker indicated by the position of the hole punched in column 8. The cards are again extracted from the stackers in the same order as before, 0 cards at the bottom and 9 cards at the top. This process is then repeated for columns 7 and 6 representing the 100's and 1,000's positions in the key. At the end of the fourth pass the cards will be in strict numerical order. It is sometimes necessary to sort cards into alphabetical order in which case, since a letter is represented by two holes punched into the same column, it is necessary to pass the cards through the machine twice on each column. For the first pass the stackers representing the top three holes are closed and the cards sorted into the 1 to 9 positions. They are then taken out in the same order as previously and passed through a second time but with the 1 to 9 stackers closed and only the first three positions open. If the cards are then removed with the contents of the first stacker on the bottom of the pack and the third on top they will now be in alphabetical order according to the first letter in the key.

It will be appreciated that off-line sorting of this kind can be a very time consuming process. While sorters can pass cards at the rate of say 1,000 a minute, a sort of 10,000 cards on a 6 digit key would entain some 60,000 card passes through the machine and allowing for handling time this would take well over an hour. For sorting large volumes of data it is quicker to write it in random order to magnetic tape and sort this on-line as described below. However, this has the disadvantage of using computer time which might be spent more advantageously in other processing. It is often the question of availability of computer time that will determine whether or not cards are pre-sorted.

Computer Sorting

A number of computer techniques are used for sorting data recorded on Magnetic Tape into a required sequence. It is not within the province of this book to describe them all in detail but the following is a description of one technique known as a two-way merge sort. In a similar way to the punched card sorting just described, the computer sort is based on a key (such as a Customer Account number) that is incorporated into each data record. The magnetic tape containing the records in random order is loaded on to a tape deck and the records are read into the central processor one group or 'Block' at a time. The number of records in a block will depend on circumstances but will be constant throughout each stage of the sorting process. For this example we will take a block size of two records which is the smallest block size that can be used for this process. The first block of two records is read from the tape into the central processor where the magnitude of the sorting keys is compared. The two records are then written out, in the sequence required, to a second magnetic tape. This means that, if the required sequence is in ascending order the record with the smallest key will be written first but if the required sequence is in descending order the record with the smallest key will be written last.

The third and fourth records on the original tape are now read into store, again compared and written out in sequence but this time to a third tape so that at this stage we have three magnetic tapes, the original input tape containing the records in random order and two new output tapes each containing one 'String' comprising two records in key sequence. From this point onwards the two output tapes will be known as tapes 1 and 2. The term 'String' is used to indicate a number of records written to an output tape in the required sequence. This process now continues until the original tape is exhausted, two records at a time being read into store, compared and written out in strings of two, alternately to tapes 1 and 2. This completes the first pass.

For the second pass, tapes 1 and 2 having been rewound, become the input tapes and a second two tapes, 3 and 4, are loaded on to decks to receive the output from the processor. This time one string of two records is read in from each of tapes 1 and 2, the four keys are compared and written out to tape 3 in correct sequence as one string of four records. The second two strings from tapes 1 and 2 are then written as a string of four to tape 4. Thus at the end of the second pass tapes 3 and 4 contain a number of four-record strings written to them alternately. For the third pass tapes 3 and 4 become the input tapes from which strings of four records are read alternately, merged into sequential strings of eight records and over-written alternately to tapes 1 and 2, now used to receive output. The eight record strings are then merged in further passes into strings of sixteen, the sixteens into strings of thirty-two and so on until one final string contains all the records in sequence. This is illustrated diagrammatically in fig. 9.2.

In the method described above, four tape decks are needed, but it is possible to manage with three by, at the end of each pass, writing the strings from the two output tapes alternately to a third tape which then becomes the one input tape for the next pass. In this case two strings are read from the one tape instead of one each from the two tapes. This, however, doubles the number of passes that need to be made to complete the sort.

Given a sufficient number of tape decks it is possible to speed up the sorting process by merging three or four strings at a time. These are known as 3-way and 4-way merge sorts, and require the use of six and eight tape decks respectively. Some other magnetic

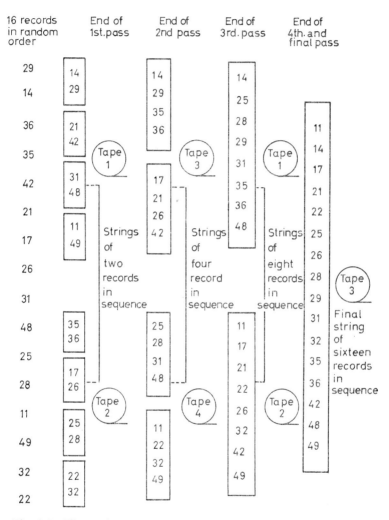

Fig. 9.2—Illustrating a two-way Merge Sort using four Tape Decks

tape sorting techniques are known as Cascade sorting, Polyphase sorting and Oscillating sorting.

It is possible to sort records into sequence by the use of the internal store of the processor alone, and this may be necessary if the configuration contains no form of backing store. However, the number of records that can be sorted in this way is limited by the size of store available to contain the records. The basic principle is to compare the keys of selected pairs of records and to exchange their position in store if the keys are not already in the sequence required. While there are different ways of selecting the pairs of records to be compared, in the example below pairs are taken in sequence starting from the first record. Thus records 1 and 2 are

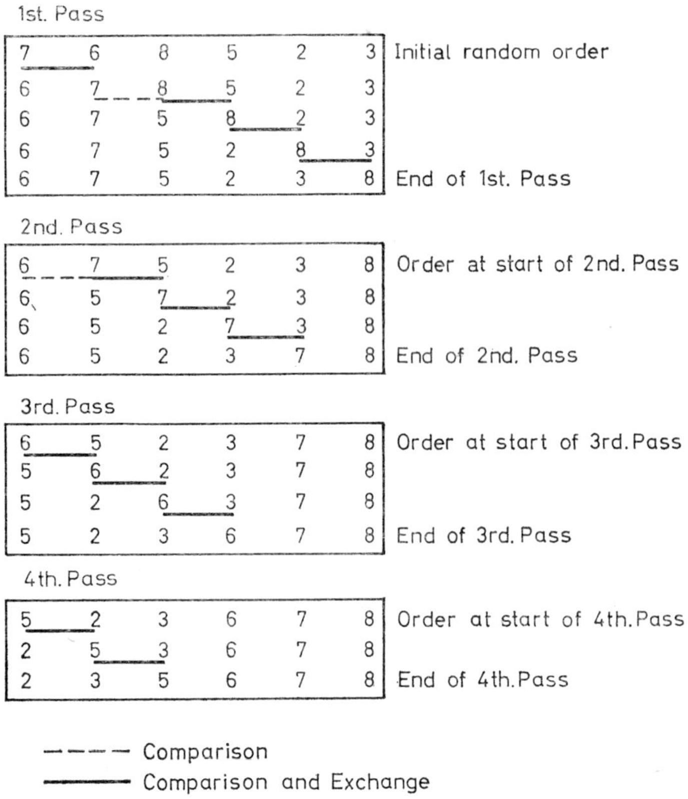

1st. Pass

7	6	8	5	2	3	Initial random order
6	7	8	5	2	3	
6	7	5	8	2	3	
6	7	5	2	8	3	
6	7	5	2	3	8	End of 1st. Pass

2nd. Pass

6	7	5	2	3	8	Order at start of 2nd. Pass
6	5	7	2	3	8	
6	5	2	7	3	8	
6	5	2	3	7	8	End of 2nd. Pass

3rd. Pass

6	5	2	3	7	8	Order at start of 3rd. Pass
5	6	2	3	7	8	
5	2	6	3	7	8	
5	2	3	6	7	8	End of 3rd. Pass

4th. Pass

5	2	3	6	7	8	Order at start of 4th. Pass
2	5	3	6	7	8	
2	3	5	6	7	8	End of 4th. Pass

— — — — Comparison

————— Comparison and Exchange

Fig. 9.3—Illustrating a Central Processor 'Exchange' Sort

compared first, then 2 and 3, then 3 and 4 and so on until the last record. This process is repeated through a number of passes until all the records are in the required sequence.

In the example illustrated in fig. 9.3 there are six records in random order indicated by the six numbers printed in the top line. The first and second records are compared, 7 and 6, and since a final sequence is required in ascending order they are exchanged with each other so that the records are now in the order indicated in the second line. The second and third records are now compared, 7 and 8, but as these are already in sequence their order is left unchanged and the next two, 8 and 5 compared. In this case they are not in sequence and so are exchanged resulting in the order shown in line 3. This comparison of adjacent records is continued until the last record is reached. At this stage the highest record key must be in the final position. The process is then repeated through a number of passes until all the records are in sequence.

CHECKS ON THE ACCURACY OF DATA

This section summarises some of the techniques that are used to ensure the accuracy of data used in computer systems. Some of them are dealt with in more detail in other chapters.

Broadly speaking, as far as the input of data to a computer is concerned, we are concerned to ensure accuracy at three stages:

(a) In the preparation of source documents
(b) In the conversion of data to an input medium
(c) In the transfer of data to the central processor and, when necessary, its subsequent transfer to another form of store.

The following techniques are commonly used:

1. Control Totals.
2. Hash or 'nonsense' totals.
3. Document sequence checks.
4. Check Digit Verification.
5. Punching Verification.
6. Parity Checks.
7. Validation.
8. Checks on reading.
9. Checks on data transfer.

Some of these checks may be used in only one of the three stages (a), (b) or (c) mentioned above while others may be applied at two or more stages.

Control Totals

Source documents are collated in batches of a convenient size. Quantitative data is pre-listed on an adding machine and a total obtained. A note of this total is included on the control slip accompanying the batch. When punched cards or punched paper tape has been prepared from the source documents the quantitative data punched into these is totalled and checked against the total from the pre-listing. See fig. 9.4. An alternative method is to punch an additional card, or field in the case of paper tape, recording the control total as a minus quantity. The sum of the data on the cards or tape should now be zero. On reading into the computer, the machine is programmed to draw the operator's attention to a batch if this zero proof is not obtained.

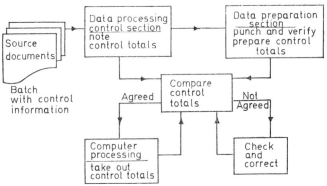

Fig. 9.4—Reconciliation of Control Totals in a Data Processing
Routine

Hash or Nonsense Totals

This consists of checking the totals of non-quantitative data taken before and after the punching process. This data may be the Account Reference Numbers, or Stock Item Numbers or indeed, the numerical value of alphabetical fields.

It should be noted that while control and hash totals ensure agreement on the total values of data recorded, they will not reveal compensating errors occurring within a particular batch of documents.

Sequence Checks

This is a check of the serial numbers on source documents to ensure they are in continuous sequence. It is usual to note the range of serial numbers on the control slip attached to the batch of documents so providing a check on continuity from one batch to another.

Check Digit Verification

This is a mathematical method of checking the validity of numerical codes appearing on documents. It means giving each reference number unique qualities so that, when subject to a series of mathematical tests, the answer is always constant. This involves adding one or two digits to the reference number in order to make it conform with the criteria demanded by the method used. These additional digits are known as Check Digits.

The system basically involves weighting each digit in the number by a pre-determined amount, the digit being either multiplied by or added to the weight. The sum of the products or the additions is then divided by a pre-determined modulus and a test made of the remainder. To meet the requirements of the test this must be a constant.

While a number of different bases are used in check digit verification it is proposed to explain only one of these in detail. This is the method most commonly used in checking reference numbers in data processing systems.

In this example, the object is to provide reference numbers which, when each digit is multiplied by a weight that increases by one for each digit from the right, gives a sum of the products exactly divisible by 11, leaving a remainder every time of zero. Example: Taking a reference number 57342, find the digit that must be added as the last figure in order to make the resultant number conform with the above principles.

1. Weight each digit by multiplying from the right by 1, 2, 3, 4, 5 etc.

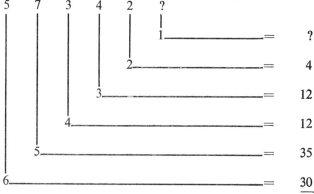

5	7	3	4	2	?	
					1 =	?
				2 =		4
			3 =			12
		4 =				12
	5 =					35
6 =						30

2. Sum of the products (excluding the final check digit)   93

3.   Divide the total 93 by the modulus $11 = 8$ remainder 5
4.   The check digit now becomes the difference between the modulus and the remainder, i.e. $11 - 5 = 6$

The reference number now becomes 57426 which conforms with these check digit verification principles, i.e. $(6 \times 1) + (2 \times 2) + (4 \times 3) + (3 \times 4) + (7 \times 5) + (5 \times 6) = 6 + 4 + 12 + 12 + 35 + 30 = 99$ which on division by 11 leaves a remainder of 0.

One disadvantage results from the use of a modulus 11. On an average, once in every ten times when the remainder is 1 the required check figure will be 10, and it may be impossible to accommodate two extra digits in the fields. In practice, when it is necessary to avoid increasing the length of the reference number by two digits, the numbers to which this applies can be discarded.

Check digit verification is carried out electronically, either in the central processor or by a Check Digit Verifier linked to say, an adding or accounting machine, so that the check is made when source documents are prepared. The types of errors arising in the transcription of numeric data are given in the table below with the percentage of errors that will be revealed using the verification system described above.

Type of Error	*Example*	*Percentage of Errors revealed*
TRANSCRIPTION	Reversing the position of digits 45678 becomes 54678 or 47658	100
TRANSCRIPTION	Mis-reading a digit and entering a different one 45678 becomes 49678	100
OMISSION	Leaving a digit out completely 45678 becomes 4678	100
ADDITION	Putting in an extra digit 45678 becomes 345678	100
RANDOM	A combination of two or more of the above 45678 becomes 9658	91

The above gives an average error finding ratio of 98·2. Assuming that an operator makes one error in every 50 entries, then this type of verification will give an accuracy ratio of 99·964%.

Verification

The verification process applied to input data is fully discussed in chapter 4.

Parity Checks

The principle of parity checking has already been discussed in relation to punched paper tape, but it should be appreciated that this form of checking is commonly applied to data held in any storage medium.

With magnetic tape, for instance, one track is reserved for parity purposes to ensure that the number of bits in each frame are either all odd or all even, and in addition the last frame in a block is used to ensure that the number of bits in each track are also either all odd or all even. Similarly, in other forms of external store and in the central processor, one bit in each word or block as appropriate, is used for parity checking.

Validation

While verification of punched cards and punched paper tape can ensure the accurate transcription of data from a source document it is no test of the accuracy of the original source data. Validation is a process of checking the validity of data against known factors, with which the data should conform. For example, Stock Item Number 1234 appearing on a document is punched and verified correctly as 1234 but we know that all Stock Item Numbers fall within the range 5000 to 5999.

Validation calls upon the program to check that all numbers fall within this range and to reject as invalid any that do not.

The general principle of validation then, is to set tolerances against which the data can be tested. It might involve the definition of a range of reference numbers or impose limits on quantitative data, for example, regarding as invalid a record of wages earned in one week in excess of £50. It is also used to check the format of a record to ensure that the right type and correct number of characters appear in a data field, that there are the correct number of fields in a data record and so on. For example, a field programmed to contain six numeric characters would be rejected as invalid if only five characters were recorded or if one was an alphabetic character. It must be emphasised, however, that validation does not check the accuracy of data but rather ensures that data items fall within predetermined limits and conform to a predetermined format.

Checks on Reading Input

Checks to guard against mis-reading data are built into the hardware of the machine, usually in the form of checking stations. These have been discussed in detail in the chapter on Input.

Checks on Data Transfer

In addition to providing parity checks in the transfer of data to and from backing stores a 'read after write' check is frequently incorporated. This entails reading the data immediately after it has been written to store and checking back to the central processor store to ensure the accuracy of the transcription. It is recognised that mechanical failure within the central processor rarely happens, but as a precaution against fault in the transfer of records a parity check is usually made.

DATA TRANSMISSION

The term, in its widest sense, refers to the transmission of data to a computer from a remote source. There are basically three ways of doing this, (a) when data is physically transported from source to the computer installation, (b) when communication lines are used to transmit to an off-line machine at the installation, and (c) when data is transmitted over communication lines as direct input to the computer.

An example of the first case is in the production of punched paper tape from, or as a by-product in the preparation of, source documents at a remote branch of an organisation. The tape is then posted or sent by messenger to the computer installation. In the second case data is transmitted over G.P.O. telephone lines from, say, a teleprinter or a punched tape reader. The data is then reproduced in punched paper tape form on an off-line punch at the computer centre and this subsequently becomes the input to the central processor.

However, the term Data Transmission is now more generally accepted as referring to the third case where data is transmitted over communication lines as direct input to the central processor. This technique of accessing the computer direct from remote terminals is known as Real Time processing. An example of this is in a banking system where the accounts of customers of local branches are processed and stored at a central computer installation. If reference is required at the branch to a customer account a request can be passed direct to the computer through an interrogating typewriter asking for details of the account. The computer will then locate the account, read the detail from the file and transmit it back to the branch.

The main factors determining which of the three methods of data transmission referred to above will be adopted are, the configuration of the computer available, the time factor and the cost. If speed is of prime importance a real time system could well be indicated, but it should be noted that this involves the use of a computer specifically designed for real time work. Among other things, direct access storage devices must be available, and since incoming messages interrupt normal processing, the computer should have the capacity for doing a number of jobs at the same time. This is particularly important if a number of remote stations are linked to the same central processor. This facility is known as Multi-programming.

SECURITY OF DATA AND FILES

As we have already seen, data may be held either in files that are stored away from the computer such as punched cards, punched paper tape, magnetic tape, exchangeable discs or magnetic cards, or in files permanently on-line to the machine such as magnetic drums, and fixed disc stores.

If magnetic storage media are stored away from the computer, particular attention must be paid to their environment. Although their magnetic state is fairly stable, care should be taken to ensure that they are not exposed to stray magnetic fields, such as those from electric motors or from cables carrying heavy currents. Excess temperature and humidity should be avoided and the air kept as dust free as far as possible. Rigid control should be exercised over the use of files, a formal record being kept of issues and receipts of each file and a history of its mechanical performance. Magnetic tape files in particular should be handled with great care, for a small mishap such as, creasing a portion of the tape could well result in the partial destruction of the magnetisable coating with the resultant loss of recorded data. It is important that the erasure of data on magnetic tapes should be controlled. A Purge Date, that is the date on or after which the data can be over-written, should be kept for each reel of tape.

In the case of direct access files where existing data is over-written during the course of processing, strict precautions must be taken to ensure that data is written to the correct locations.

Facilities should exist for the reconstruction of all types of file in the event of complete or partial accidental destruction. The method used will be determined by the type of file and the method of processing. For example, in a magnetic tape system where master files are held and up-dated by movement tapes, if the previous master file and up-dating tapes are retained, the current master file can be reconstructed if necessary. As an additional safeguard, three generations of file are frequently kept. An example using direct access files, is the periodic copying of the whole file on to magnetic tape, and the retention of the movement files subsequent to copying. This again provides sufficient information to reconstruct the current file in the event of its destruction. There is one final point.

The complete collection of computer records constitutes an enormous investment in programming and processing. It is impossible to adequately insure an organisation against the disruption which would be caused if they were entirely destroyed, say by a fire or an explosion. To guard against this hazard, copies of all files should be stored at a place remote from the computer installation.

EXERCISES CHAPTER 9

1. What information would you expect to be held in a record of a customer's account on a Sales Ledger master file. Suggest the contents of two types of record that would be used to up-date the master file.

2. A Stores Requisition is received by the control section of the D.P. Department holding data recording issues from store. Trace the progress of the data until the time it is held on magnetic tape ready for up-dating a Stock Inventory master file, mentioning any accuracy checks you think would be made during its progress.

3. Distinguish between (a) Verification and (b) Validation. A data field may be verified as correct but rejected as invalid. Why?

4. Calculate the digit that must be added to the following reference numbers to make then conform to a Check Digit Verification system using a weighting 1, 2, 3, 4, ... and a modulus 11. 4963, 5633, 7100, 8368.

5. What do you understand by the following:
   (a) Key,   (b) Hash Totals,   (c) Parity.

6. Information to be processed in a computer is delivered to the punch room for card preparation in batches.
   What purpose does this batching serve?
   What do you understand by Hash and Control totals. When are they first derived and for what are they used?
   (Royal Society of Arts—Computer Appreciation—Stage I)

7. What precautions would you take against:
   (a) Complete destruction of data files by fire, and
   (b) The accidental erasure of a series of records on a master file.

8. Describe how a series of records, stored in random order on a magnetic tape, could be sorted into key number sequence using three decks only.

9. In preparing a source document the reference number 4636 is entered incorrectly as 436G, and the account number 83720 entered as 87320. On punching the value £87·63 is mis-read by both the punching and the verifying operators as £89·63. Explain how you would expect these errors to be found.

10. Discuss the following statement. 'It does not matter if mistakes are made in source documents, the computer will find them.' •

11. An order form contains two types of data.
    (i) Product numbers—which are fixed identification codes.
    (ii) Quantities ordered—which are the amounts ordered by customers and clearly are not fixed by nature.

    Explain two methods, one for each of these types of data, which could be employed so that a computer could be programmed to detect a large proportion of the errors liable to occur as a result of transcribing the data on to a computer input medium.
    Illustrate each method with a simple example showing how a single transcription error would be detected.
    (Institute of Data Processing)

10

Systems Design and Implementation

While it is impractical to discuss in just one chapter all the implications in the design and implementation of computer systems, the object of this section is to give an overall picture of the stages and procedures involved up to the point when the system is ready for programming.

It would be as well to mention at the outset that different schools of thought exist on the basic approaches to Systems Analysis and Design. One suggests that a very detailed investigation of present systems at all levels of staff is necessary in order to bring to light what the output objectives really are and exactly what procedures are required to attain them. Another suggests that, having formulated objectives at top management level, a standard computer system can be 'bought in' as a package deal, disregarding to a great extent the detail of existing practices, while a third compromises between the two by formulating overall objectives and fills in the detail by a process of investigation. Doubtless all of these have their place in different circumstances.

As mentioned in an earlier chapter, in any organisation systems already exist in one form or another for the processing of data, before the decision to use a computer is taken. These systems have probably grown up over a long period of time with the development of the organisation to meet its particular requirements, and have been modified as the requirements have changed and as the volumes of data to be processed have increased. Also, in all probability, the systems have developed within a departmental structure, individual procedures being geared to meet the requirements of particular departments, and so have a tendency to exist in isolation. This means that a variety of data processing methods are used within the organisation involving, in varying degrees, a combination of manual and machine methods. Serious consideration of the desirability of introducing computer systems is often triggered off by management's realisation of the inadequacies inherent in this kind of situation.

Between the initial consideration of a computer installation and the time the systems become fully operational on the machine, a great deal of detailed work is necessary. This may be classified into the following areas:

1. An initial survey to see if it is worth while to change to computer methods. This is usually known as a Feasibility Study and it will form the basis on which the decision is made.
2. The investigation into, and analysis of, present systems and procedures.
3. The design and detailed specification of systems in a form suitable for computer processing.
4. Constructing and encoding the programs required to operate the systems.
5. Implementation of the new systems.

FEASIBILITY STUDY

In the early days of computers, it was often not so much a question of assessing if it was worth while to introduce a computer but rather of seeing if the computer itself was able to do the job. With modern machines this question rarely arises, and we are more concerned with whether the use of a computer is justified. From this point of view, perhaps a better term for this initial study is a Justification Study rather than a Feasibility Study. While it would be safe to say that computer processing for all forms of commercial data is feasible, it might well be that the benefits accruing from the introduction of a machine do not justify the high expense and considerable re-organisation involved.

Whatever we call this exercise, however, the main object is to ensure that a change over to computer methods is a workable project and is economically viable. Now the criteria on which the decision is based will vary from situation to situation. In one, expense may be the critical factor, in another time might be of prime importance and expense secondary, while other points of judgement may centre around staff shortage, accuracy, supply of management information and so on. Within the framework of a feasibility study, it is suggested that information could well be required on the following points to enable an objective decision to be reached by management:

1. The overall objectives that will be attained, in terms of areas of work absorbed and the information that will be generated from the systems.

2. The improvements that will result over present methods in accuracy, availability and control of data.
3. The provision of adequate information for management control purposes. Will it place in the hands of management the information to enable it to run the whole organisation more efficiently?
4. Estimate of cost. This involves a cost evaluation of both present methods and the projected computer methods to provide a comparison, taking into account direct costs and any indirect savings that may accrue.
5. The effect on the organisation generally, including changes that will have to be made in departmental organisation and in areas of managerial responsibility. The probable effect on staffing with an estimate of possible redundancies and the need for re-training.
6. An estimate of the date by which the machine is expected to be installed and the systems to become operational. A computer is not the immediate answer to a current problem. It will probably be between twelve and eighteen months from the time the decision is made to buy that the first computer runs are made. The manufacturer's delivery date does not necessarily determine the implementation date. Time must be allowed for the development of systems and the necessary re-organisation.
7. How long can the machine be expected to give reasonable service? Change is costly and can be upsetting while it is happening. After the widespread change resulting from the initial conversion, no further major upheavals should be entertained for some time. Are there any technical developments round the corner that will make the processing techniques decided upon redundant or uneconomic in the near future?

SYSTEMS INVESTIGATION

Having made the decision to go ahead on the basis of such a feasibility study, the next stages to set in motion are the detailed investigations of existing systems and the design of the new computer systems. This is known as a Systems Project, covering two main areas of work, Systems Analysis and Systems Design. Analysis is concerned with the investigation of the present position, fact finding, and recording the information found in such a way that a clear and precise picture is built up of what is going on. From this process, information is derived to help in the development of the new computer systems. Systems design is concerned with working out how the required objectives of the systems can be achieved in the most effective way, and specifying in detail all the processes involved.

FACT FINDING

Of the activities investigated by the systems analysts, he will be interested in the What, Where, Why, How, When and Who of the situation, and further than this, he will not only be concerned with what is actually happening but also with what should happen according to company practice and policy. There is quite often an appreciable difference between the two.

A number of techniques are used to find the facts of a situation,

(a) the examination of records, documents, files, organisation charts, and procedure manuals,

(b) personal observation of staff as they carry out their work,

(c) getting staff to complete questionnaires and

(d) personal interviews and discussion with staff.

It is usually this last method that figures most prominently in a systems investigation.

The information the analyst is looking for can be classified under the following headings:

1. Objectives. What is the system or procedure trying to achieve?

2. Output. In what specific form are the outputs communicated, what are the contents of each? Is the output used and if so for what purpose and who by? Is it suitable for the purpose required and, indeed, is it really necessary at all? Is the same information being processed as the output of another procedure? Does the output of this procedure become the input of another?

3. Input. What is the input? What forms does it take? Where does it come from? Is it the output of another procedure? Are all input records treated in the same way or are there exceptions? What is the detailed content of the Input?

4. Records and Files. What files are kept? How often are they brought up to date? What purpose do they serve? How long are files kept before being disposed of?

5. Processing. What is done to convert specific input information into the required output? Are any special skills required? How often is each procedure carried out? Could the job be done better if input was in a different form? Does processing anticipate further processes later on?

6. Volumes and Growth. What are current volumes? Are there any peak periods or seasonal fluctuations? What has been the rate of growth over the last two or three years? Is continued growth anticipated?

7. Environments. What is the context within which the system operates? This will include research into the organisational structure of the departments involved, the adequacy of staff in terms of both numbers and performance, communications within the department and with other departments and the degree of reliance on other services within the organisation. A further important factor is to ascertain company policy in relation to the particular functions being investigated and any other factors such as trade practices and legal requirements that must be taken into account.

8. Exceptions. Are there any exceptions to the general processing routine? If so, is it possible to classify them so as to bring them in to line for machine processing?

9. Controls. What controls exist over the accuracy of the processing of the data processed?

In addition to these details relating to the procedures in the processing of the systems, there are four other things that the analyst will be interested in. These are:

(a) the equipment that is already in use, accounting machines, calculating machines and so on.

(b) estimating the cost of running the system under current methods, to provide a basis for comparison with the cost of any new methods proposed.

(c) the deadlines that have to be met by the output of the system and particularly why outputs have to be produced by these times.

(d) Which members of staff are responsible for making decisions, what type of decisions they are expected to make and the criteria upon which these decisions are based.

Fact finding, then, is the process of finding out how data is being processed within the organisation. It enables the Systems Analyst to build up a picture of detailed requirements and ensures that he is conversant with all of the factors that must be taken into consideration when re-designing the system.

FACT RECORDING AND ANALYSIS

Information obtained during a systems investigation must be methodically recorded. It is usual to open a Systems Investigation File in which is kept copies of all documents relating to the system and the notes made by the Analyst during his enquiries.

A number of methods that are used for recording and analysing facts are suggested below. While the circumstances of the situation and the individual preference of the analyst concerned will influence the recording techniques used, there are two basic factors that should be borne in mind. The first of these is that the object is to set down in a clear and concise form all of the facts that are relevant to the situation so that they can be referred to and understood during the design phase. The second is that the records in the systems file should be understandable by everyone concerned in the investigation, not just the analyst writing up the record. To this end, while there are no generally accepted standards, most firms using electronic data processing techniques extensively, evolve their own standard procedures for documenting systems so that should there be a change in personnel working on any particular project the problems of handing over are minimised.

Information Flow Diagrams

These are usually in the form of Block or Flow charts. The aim of this type of chart is to show the logical sequence of events that take place. Use is made of symbols representing activities, connected by flow-lines. A short description of the activity is contained in the symbol with, if necessary, additional explanatory notes appended. Block and Flow charts are considered in more detail in chapter 8.

Procedure Narrative

This is an organised descriptive account of procedures in a very detailed form. Usually it contains three basic elements

OPERATOR	OPERATION	OPERAND
Who does it	What is done	On what is it done

Organisation Chart

This shows the organisational structure of the departments responsible for carrying out the functions being investigated and defines areas of responsibility. This type of chart often also includes the numbers of staff engaged in each type of activity.

Document Flow Chart

This is a graphical presentation of the flow of documents and the procedures they are subjected to from the time they originate until they are eventually filed away. The detail should include the number of copies raised, how these are distributed and what happens to each copy.

Cost Tables

In order to give a breakdown of operating costs of a system or a department, tables can be constructed analysing costs under main headings. The main cost factors usually involved are, staff, supplies, equipment and the cost of accommodation. These in turn can be broken down in terms of the procedures within the department or system.

Document Description Form

This contains a brief description of the document for identification purposes, a detailed record of the data appearing on the document with minimum and maximum size of data fields where applicable. It should indicate how the document originates, the volumes processed during a given period (with any periodic fluctuations) and how often the documents are processed (daily, weekly, or monthly). Finally it should state the use to which the document is put, for example, for up-dating a master record, or for distribution to customers.

SYSTEMS DESIGN

The general considerations in the design of systems are as follows:
1. To generate the required information to the desired degree of accuracy, when needed, and in the form required.
2. To be as flexible as possible. The system must be capable of change within a limited range as may be necessary with changing conditions and changing volumes. In other words, the system must not go to pieces if minor changes are made.
3. As economical as possible. The analysts are not concerned with just one system in isolation but with the processing needs of the organisation as a whole. The same inputs and outputs may be common to two or more systems. For example, an Advice note could be the source document for the preparation of Sales Invoices in a Sales Ledger System and also for Stock Issues in a Stock Inventory system. The same consideration applies to

output documents and to files. The analyst will be concerned with the cost of recording source data, its preparation in machine input form and the cost of computer processing time.

4. Control requirements. The system must contain checks which will ensure the accuracy and security of data at all stages and have the capability of measuring its performance against the planned objectives. It should also be as 'fool proof' as possible so that no one person's mistakes will easily disorganise the system.

5. Exception Handling. Should there be any exceptions to the general routine of processing the analysts must decide how these should be treated. While a system could be designed to deal with all exceptions, this would not necessarily be the most efficient or most economical way of dealing with them. Consideration should be given to processing exceptions manually.

6. Effective Document Design. A document is the vehicle for conveying information, and must be designed to do this in the most effective way.

7. Effective Coding Design. Records processed by a computer are usually recognised by a 'key'. Coding systems should be designed so that the main activity to which the key relates is easily identifiable and so that the keys can be checked for accuracy.

8. Constraints and Legal requirements. Within an organisation there are usually factors which over-ride purely internal systems considerations. These must be taken into account in systems design, even though they may make the system more involved than would otherwise be necessary. Such factors might include practices agreed with Trade Unions, custom and usage within a particular industry and, indeed, facets of management policy. All these impose constraints within which the analyst must work. In particular, when designing a system, allowance must be made for audit requirements and to this end, the analyst will find it necessary to consult with the firms auditors while developing his systems in order to ascertain their requirements.

The situation as it now stands is that the objectives towards which we are to work have been specified in the feasibility study, information has been gleaned on the existing situation and more detail on the requirements of the system has been obtained through the process of fact finding and analysis. In addition to this we have a number of general considerations that have to be borne in mind.

We must now consider the development of an automatic data processing system to replace the old manual methods. While a number of stages in the design of a system are given later, two points should first be emphasised. One of these is that systems investigation and systems design are not completely consecutive activities in the sense that all of the fact finding and recording is finished before the design stage is commenced. While the analyst will usually make a start with investigating existing methods, continual reference back for additional information is necessary during the course of designing. Secondly, the design of a system tends to progress through a series of levels, each succeeding level specifying the requirements in greater detail until eventually a final and completely detailed systems definition is produced.

The following section breaks down the systems development procedure into a number of areas of work and presents them in the order in which they would probably be tackled by the analyst.

Output Specification

By this time we will know in principle what is required of the system; this will have been decided upon at the feasibility study stage. If, for example, we are concerned with a stock inventory system, one of the outputs required could well be a list of goods to be re-ordered. At this stage in the systems design we are concerned with deciding the information that this list should contain. It may be, for instance that the list is to be passed on to a purchasing department where the orders are raised manually. In this case the output record content might consist only of an identification of the item, a statement of current stock, re-order level and re-order quantity. On the other hand a completely automated re-ordering systems may have been decided upon, which will print out the purchase orders direct on the computer printer. In this case additional output information such as the name and address of the supplier would be required. Not only are we interested at this stage in the content of the records, but also in the order in which they must be produced, e.g. item number order, priority for ordering, product group order and so on. We also need to specify the frequency with which the reports are to be compiled and what is going to happen to them after they have been prepared.

File Design

Having decided output requirements, we now have to decide the files that are needed to produce this information. Since, by this stage, the hardware that will be available will have been decided upon, the type of file available (magnetic tape, magnetic disc etc.) will be known. It remains to specify the content of the records kept on file, the sequence in which these are to be stored, the anti-cipated number of records in each file and the frequency with which the files will be processed.

Input Specification

Next we are concerned with the input data necessary to generate the information on file that will in turn produce the output reports. As we saw earlier in the chapter on Data Preparation, this is usually a two stage matter, first recording the data at source and then converting it to a machine input form. For source documents the method of originating the data and recording it at source will have to be decided, the content of the input record, the controls that are to be imposed to ensure accuracy, and the routine for forwarding the documents to the D.P. Department for processing. As far as the conversion is concerned, here again a routine must be defined for preparing the data, controls established to ensure accuracy during conversion and the procedure for creating or up-dating files from the input medium outlined.

Procedure Specification

This is concerned with working out the procedures necessary throughout the whole system, manual and machine, in order to produce the required outputs. While there are recognised methods for recording procedures (Block Charts, Flow Charts, Narrative etc.), there are no firm rules that can be applied to the actual procedure development process. This relies on the experience and aptitude of the analyst and his ability to bring creative and logical thinking to bear on the solution of the problems inherent in systems design. It is, to a certain extent, a process of trial and error—formulating a possible solution, testing this against known conditions, modifying and adjusting it if requirements are not met until eventually a satisfactory final solution is found.

Input and Output Form Design

Having decided the content of source, input and output records, we are next concerned with the detailed design of the documents to contain the information. Source data is usually recorded on pre-printed forms. Design of these should take into account the next stage, that of data preparation, forms being designed so that data fields appear in the most convenient order for transcription to punched cards or punched paper tape. It is often as well, to ensure efficient recording at source, to specify on the source document the size, or maximum size of each data field, the type of field—alphabetic or numeric—and to incorporate any explanatory notes that are considered necessary for the guidance of the person completing the form. In addition to this, any non-variable data can be included when the form is initially printed. If machine input is punched cards, the cards will have to be printed showing fields and titles of fields to conform with the data appearing in the source document. However, whatever the input form the format of the input record must at this stage be clearly defined.

Much the same factors apply to the design of forms to contain output reports many of which, if the output is by way of a line-printer, can be pre-printed. The layout of data, position of fields within the output record, and size and content of fields must be clearly defined and communicated to the processor through the program, to control the format of the output reports.

RECORDING A NEW SYSTEM

Having designed a new system as suggested above, the whole must be recorded formally and in detail. This formal record of the system is known as a system specification or a system definition. This should contain the following information:

(a) An overall description of the system, listing the inputs, outputs and files, and outlining the procedures involved and the aims of the system.
(b) A detailed specification of input, output and file records, accompanied by appropriate charts, specimen documents and explanations.
(c) A detailed account of all procedures again with appropriate charts and notes.
(d) For the guidance of programmers, a specification of each program required to operate the procedures.
(e) Details of how the system is to be implemented, specifying exactly how the change-over from the original manual system should be done.
(f) A note of the equipment needed to operate the system, not only for the actual computer processing and data preparation, but also any ancillary machines needed in the course of the preparation of source data and for dealing with output reports.
(g) Specification of testing procedures and test data for the programs and the system.

Finally, the complete systems specification should be formally agreed by management. After this the final stage is the implementation of the system.

SYSTEMS IMPLEMENTATION

Since many of the problems associated with the initial setting up of a computer department are discussed in other chapters, we will consider implementation procedures on the assumption that a new system is being taken on to an already existing computer department. This will be considered under four main headings, Staff Training, Pre-take-on procedures, File Conversion and the actual change-over process from the original manual methods.

Staff Training

Assuming the operations staff of the computer department to have been already trained, we are concerned with the problem of training those people outside the computer installation who will be involved in operating the new system. This includes both those who are concerned with the recording of source data and any manual processing this gives rise to, and also those who are going to use the output reports generated by the system. Some of the staff concerned will already have a good idea of what is going on as they will have been involved in the investigation and design stages of the project, but now it becomes necessary to give all the staff concerned a complete account of how the new system will operate, and individual members of staff a detailed explanation of what their particular role will be. This is not just a question of issuing instructions to everyone concerned, but also of enlisting their co-operation by involving them in the system and explaining the benefits that can be expected both to themselves and the company as a whole.

Perhaps the best approach is by personal discussion between the analyst responsible for designing the system and the staff who will work with it, with special discussions at supervisory and middle management level.

Specific training must be given to those people concerned in operating the new procedures to ensure that they are familiar with the new documentation, how documents are to be completed, what controls and checks are to be imposed and when information is to be forwarded to the computer department for processing. Not only should verbal explanations be made and demonstrations given, but the whole of the information should be collated in the form of a Procedure manual, specifying in detail how each procedure is to be carried out and providing specimen forms with explanations as to their use. These procedure manuals must be made readily available to those members of staff concerned with carrying out the work.

Pre-Take-on Procedures

These are concerned with making the physical arrangements necessary for implementing the new system. The introduction of new methods will usually involve a degree of re-organisation in offices, stores and so on. Adequate supplies of the new stationery and forms must be made available, and arrangements made to dispose of old files and forms no longer required. It may be necessary to provide additional machines both at the source data recording stage and at the computer output stage. For example, adding machines may be needed to prepare pre-lists for control totals, or where documents for distribution direct to customers have not previously been produced, a folding machine may be necessary.

File Conversion

This is the process of transferring the information required for the system, from the old manual files to the new computer files.

The two major factors to bear in mind in file conversion are firstly the large volume of work to be done in a comparatively short time, and secondly the fact that records on files are not static but are continually being modified by records of business activity. It is hardly practical to stop all business activity while the conversion process is taking place. To help cope with the high volume of work it is often a sound policy either to engage temporary staff or to switch staff temporarily from other less pressing activities. For the conversion of the file records to punched card or punched paper tape form, the aid of a punching bureau can be enlisted.

The second complication, that of continually changing records, can be met by a two-stage conversion process. The first stage takes on the non-variable content of the records, which usually represents the bulk of the data, and then the variable content, a much shorter job, is taken on as the second stage. This means that the original files can still be up-dated while the conversion of non-variable data is taking place.

As an example of this, consider a stock inventory record containing the following information:

Stock Item Number
Description
Minimum Stock
Maximum Stock
Re-order Quantity
Unit Price
Quantity
Value

The first five data fields could well be taken on to the new files during the first stage since these are not likely to change in the short term, and then in the second stage the last three fields together with the stock item number for a second time, in order to marry-up the two parts of the record.

A file conversion routine usually consists of three stages. First comes the preparation of a document from the original file record, to be used for punching, second the preparation in punched card form, and third the computer runs to create the new files.

CHANGE-OVER PROCEDURES

There are three approaches to the change-over to the new computer procedures.

Parallel Running

This means that, for a period, data is processed by both the old and the new methods. Results of the two are compared and the old method discontinued as soon as the new one is proved.

Pilot Running

In this case, the new method is proved with simulated or old data while current data is being processed by the old system. Using old data that has been previously processed manually has the advantage that the results of processing are already known and can be checked against the output of the new system. When the new system has been thoroughly tested and proved a switch is made, discontinuing the old procedures and operating the new.

There is, however, a second type of pilot running which consists of the gradual take-on of a system procedure by procedure. This, of course, is only viable with a system that lends itself to this piece-meal absorption. As each procedure is taken over, the output is fed back compared and used in the old system until progressively the whole system has been taken over.

Direct Change-over

This means the closing down of the old system completely and starting up the new as soon as possible afterwards. It does not provide the safeguards of Parallel and Pilot running and is normally only used when there is insufficient similarity between old and new methods to provide a comparison. A direct change-over usually has to be implemented during a break in normal business activities, for example, at holiday time or a week-end.

EXERCISES CHAPTER 10

1. What do you understand by a 'Feasibility Study'. Suggest the main factors on which you would report when carrying out such a study?

2. Discuss the techniques you would use in obtaining information about the operation of present systems in a company, with a view to using this information to help design new computer systems.

3. What are the main stages in the design of a new system for computer application?

4. The systems analyst must incorporate into his system, checks to ensure as high a degree of accuracy as possible. Suggest some of the methods he will use to do this.

5. What are the main aims a systems analyst has in mind when designing a new computer system.

6. Explain the three main ways of changing over from a manual system to a system processed by computer.

7. Describe a routine for converting records held on file in a manual system to a magnetic tape file.

8. Draw up a check list of the activities involved in designing and implementing a computer system.

9. What information would you expect to find in a 'Systems Definition'?

10. List and comment briefly on the main activities in the design of a computer system to replace an existing manual system, placing these in the order you think they should be dealt with.

(Institute of Data Processing)

11

The Nature and Purpose of Programs

As we saw when discussing Central Processors in chapter 6, a Computer Program is a series of instructions that are executed by the machine in order to carry out a required procedure. Programming is the process of writing, compiling and assembling this list of instructions.

INSTRUCTION CODES

The instructions are stored in the central processor, where they are worked through in sequence and the appropriate operations carried out. In the central processor store, each instruction takes on a standard form, known as an Instruction Format, and occupies a fixed-size group of binary positions (usually a complete word). Thus each instruction is individually addressable. In most machines, storage locations can hold either program instructions or data, but in contrast to data, the instructions must be stored in the sequence in which they are to be performed. This does not mean that they must necessarily occupy a single block of consecutive locations, but the last instruction in one series of addresses must direct to the first in the next series. (See fig. 11.1).

We need not consider the detailed construction of an instruction format, as these vary from computer to computer, but knowledge of the basic elements is important. Essentially an instruction has two parts. The first part determines the operation the computer is to perform, and is known as the Function or Operation element of the instruction. The second specifies the factors on which the function is to be performed, by quoting the addresses at which these factors are located. This is known as the Address element. The function element is common to all instruction formats irrespective of the type of computer, but the address element may quote one, two, or three locations depending on the type of machine. Examples of these are given in the chapter on central processors. For the purpose of illustrating the points made in this chapter, we will use a single-

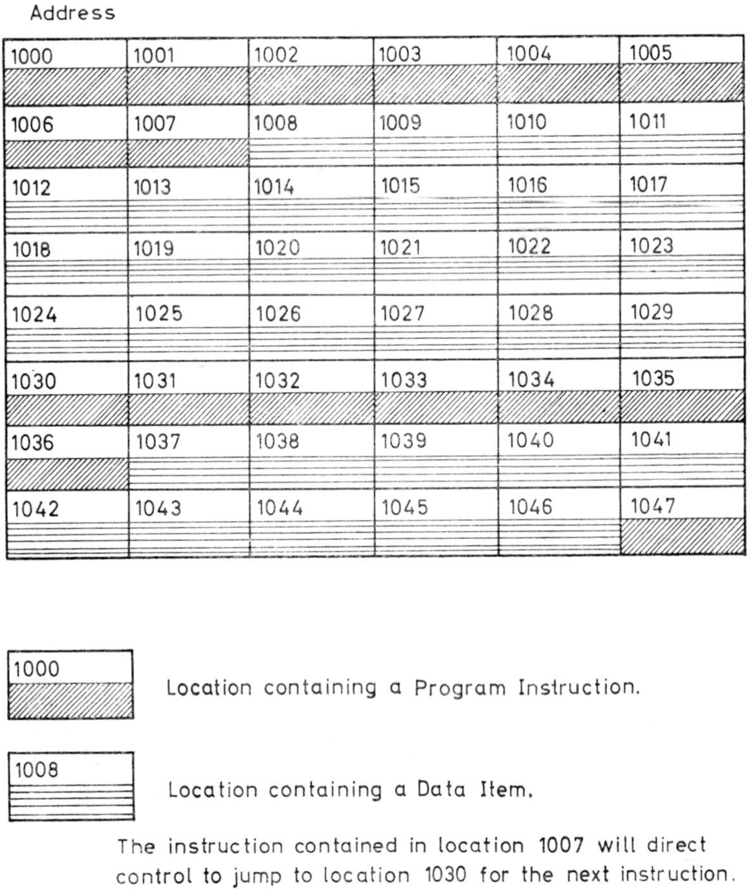

Address

1000	1001	1002	1003	1004	1005
1006	1007	1008	1009	1010	1011
1012	1013	1014	1015	1016	1017
1018	1019	1020	1021	1022	1023
1024	1025	1026	1027	1028	1029
1030	1031	1032	1033	1034	1035
1036	1037	1038	1039	1040	1041
1042	1043	1044	1045	1046	1047

Location containing a Program Instruction.

Location containing a Data Item.

The instruction contained in location 1007 will direct control to jump to location 1030 for the next instruction.

Fig. 11.1—Storage of Program and Data in the Central Processor

address format consisting of three elements, an accumulator address, a function and a location address.

Whatever the instruction format, the instructions are stored in binary form in the central processor. It would be a far too laborious a procedure for the programmer to write the instructions in binary, and so ordinary decimal digits can be used for this purpose. These, on being punched into cards or paper tape in the same way as data can be read into store and converted into binary in the process.

As far as the function is concerned, the computer hardware is constructed to perform only a limited number of basic instructions. This list of instructions together with the alphabetic or numeric coding that must be communicated to the machine to instruct it to perform a given instruction, is known as a Function Code, an Order Code or sometimes as an Operations Code.

An instruction to multiply together the contents of location 2345 and the contents of accumulator 2, could take this form:

3	2	2345
Function Code	Address of	Address of the
for 'Multiply'	Accumulator	Location

An instruction compiled in this way is usually known as a Computer Instruction Code or a Machine Code. It represents the basic form of instruction that the central processor has been designed to recognise and execute. It uses an absolute address, that is the actual location number of the address in which the data is stored and for this reason is sometimes referred to as Absolute Coding.

If we think again about the 'function' part of the instruction, we can see that while the use of numbers to indicate functions has the advantage of being directly recognisable by the machine, from the programmer's point of view it is not particularly convenient. It means that he has either to remember, or to refer to a list for, the numeric coding for each function he wants to write into his program. Things would obviously be easier if the function code bore some resemblance to the function description. In the early days of programming this led to the use of alphabetic codes that could be recognised in themselves as a function, and this form of code is known as a Mnemonic (from the Greek word for memory) code. There is no standard Mnemonic code common to all machines, as each manufacturer developed his own, but the general principle was to relate the code to the function so that, for example, 'multiply' might become MULT, 'transfer' TRAN, 'add' ADD, and so on. In this code the above example would be written:

MULT	2	2345
Mnemonic function	Accumulator	Data
code for 'multiply'	address	address

The problem that now arises is that we are trying to communicate with the machine in a language it is unable to understand. To the machine, 'multiply' is '3', to the programmer it is MULT. A converting mechanism must therefore be provided to change one to the other. To save getting bogged down in terminology at this point we will avoid giving this process a name but will come back to it later. However, what we have done is to establish in principle that if we want to communicate with the machine in any way other than by using the basic machine code, a conversion process will be necessary.

If we turn our attention to the 'address' part of the instruction as it was previously described, we notice that the same consideration applies to this as to the 'function' part; the addresses themselves bear no relation to the description of what is stored in them. Specifying the locations as 'absolute' addresses also has the disadvantage that the programmer must keep a register of all locations, with a note of what they contain. For example, if he allocates a data item called 'Cash' to location 4567, he must note this so that he does not use the same location for another data item, and so that he knows where 'Cash' is to be found should he want to refer to it again later. All this could be avoided if the programmer could, in the 'address' part of the instruction, quote the *name* of the data item rather than the address at which it was stored. Using a mnemonic code for the address as well as the function can result in an instruction of the form:

      MULT   2   CASH

in which we use a 'symbolic' address instead of an absolute address. When this type of coding is used in program instructions, it is known as an Assembly Code, or less frequently as a Pseudocode. A programmer writing in this form is said to be using an Assembly or a Pseudo Computer Language.

ASSEMBLING INSTRUCTION CODES

When symbolic addresses are used, the allocation of storage space for data items in the central processor, and the translation from the symbolic to the absolute addresses are left to the computer itself. Once again a converting function must be interposed between the assembly code and the instructions which the central processor can actually use. Now if we were translating from one language to another, say from English to Spanish, we would probably make use of an English/Spanish dictionary. The same principle applies to the conversion of an Assembly computer language to a Machine computer language, but the name we give to the conversion mechanism is an ASSEMBLER PROGRAM. Unlike a dictionary, however, its function need not be limited to word for word (or in this case, instruction for instruction) translating. An assembler program could well perform all the following functions:

1. Translate a function mnemonic into the machine language equivalent.
2. Translate symbolic addresses into absolute addresses.
3. Assemble machine instructions into the required machine format.
4. Allocate storage areas.
5. Index symbolic addresses against absolute addresses.

At this point, two other terms must be introduced. The first of these is SOURCE program. A source program is one written by a programmer using a computer language as distinct from a machine language. The second new term is OBJECT program, which refers to the program after it has been converted or ASSEMBLED into a machine code. It must be emphasised that these two terms, source program and object program refer to the same program but at different stages in its preparation. The first stage is prepared by the programmer, but the second by the machine itself.

The process of converting a source program into an object program by the use of an assembler program can be performed in two ways. One way is to read into and to hold in store the whole of both the source and the assembler programs. As each source program instruction is accessed, reference is made to the assembler program, a conversion made to a machine coded instruction and the instruction executed. The machine then proceeds to the next source program instruction, converts and executes this, and so on until the program has been completed. The use of an assembler program in this way is known as INTERPRETING. However, a more usual way is to make a complete conversion run. This means that the assembler program is stored in the central processor, the source program is read in instruction by instruction, converted into machine code and these machine coded instructions are written out to some form of storage, say magnetic tape. This gives a permanent object program that can in turn be read into store for processing data as required. This method is known as TRANSLATING (illustrated in fig. 11.2). In this case both the assembler and the source programs are written to magnetic tape and the computer output, the object program, written to a third magnetic tape.

In the use of assembly languages we have not departed very far from the basic machine instruction; in fact, all we have done is to substitute mnemonics for numbers in the instructions, thus making things a little easier for the programmer and relieving him

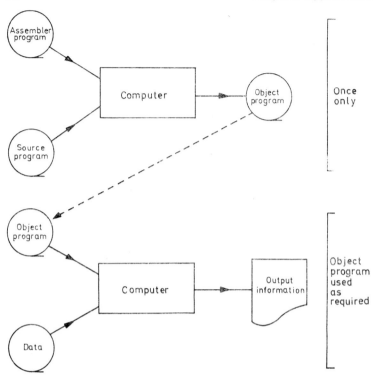

Fig. 11.2—Assembling a Source Program

of some of the donkey-work such as allocating and recording storage locations. However, the program still uses the same number of instructions as a machine code program, and the instruction format remains basically the same. The first of these two considerations leads to the use of the term MICRO-INSTRUCTION for this type of instruction, that is, one which bears a one to one relationship with the machine code. The second, the use of a language whose, format is still directly related to the machine instruction format, gives rise to the description of this type of language as 'MACHINE-ORIENTATED.'

PROGRAMMING LANGUAGES

We can now go a stage further. From the programmer's point of view programming would be very much simplified if we could make one instruction in the source program generate a number of instructions in the object program, and if, rather than keeping to the machine instruction format we could use ordinary English language phrases.

A number of computer languages have been developed which meet these two requirements to a greater or lesser extent. The term given to a source program instruction that will generate a number of object program instructions is a MACRO-INSTRUCTION; that is, it bears a one for many relationship to the machine code in contrast to the one for one relationship of a micro-instruction.

Computer languages using macro-instructions and written in a form more closely resembling English language statements or mathematical statements than a machine code does, are called PROBLEM-ORIENTATED languages or AUTOCODES. We said earlier that a number of such languages have been developed. There are some, developed by manufacturers, which can only be used on their own machines, but there are three that have been developed for general use on any machine. These are COBOL (Common Business Orientated Language), FORTRAN (Formula TRANslator) and ALGOL (ALGOrithmic Language), and they will be described in a little more detail later in the chapter.

COMPILING PROGRAMMING LANGUAGES

As we saw earlier, the use of symbolic instructions in mnemonic codes involves the use of an assembler program to convert the instructions into machine language. It is evident that a far more complicated device will be required to convert a program written in a problem-orientated language into machine instructions. The program for doing this is known as a COMPILER. This is a program containing a list of the statements used in the problem-orientated language, and for each statement a list of the machine instructions necessary to perform the statement. Thus by running the source (problem-orientated) program with the compiler program, an object (machine instruction) program is produced. This object program is then used to process the data. It will be appreciated that since different types of machine have different machine code formats, each type of machine must have its own individual compiler program to convert the computer language into the correct machine code.

To summarise, then, a computer program consists of a number of instructions assembled together into a logical sequence according to defined rules. On being executed by the computer, these instructions will cause it to carry out a predetermined procedure. There are various levels of computer language in which programs can be written. First, the language which uses the actual numeric codes and instruction format on which the machine itself operates. This us usually known as a machine language. Second, the type of language which substitutes mnemonics for the numeric coding. These are sometimes known as Symbolic languages, sometimes as Pseudo-languages, but are generally classified as 'low-level' languages. Finally there are the computer languages which more nearly approach ordinary written language, and which do not conform to the machine instruction format. These 'problem-orientated' languages are generally known as 'high-level' languages.

It should be made clear that the levels of language are not quite as distinct as the above classification might suggest. Some languages for specific machines have elements of both low and high level languages in them, having most instructions written on a one for one basis but also having the power to use macro-instructions for some specific purposes, e.g. for input and output routines.

Now we can return to consider the three high-level languages mentioned above: Cobol, Fortran and Algol.

COBOL

(COmmon Business-Orientated Language) is an international language developed for commercial use. It can be used on any computer having sufficient central processor storage capacity and for which a compiler can be prepared. It is a problem-orientated language using statements written in simple English that can be associated with the normal terms used in business applications. It has the advantage, in common with other high-level languages, that it is not necessary for the programmer to have a detailed knowledge of the computer's machine code.

A Cobol program contains four parts. These are:
>Identification division
>Environment division
>Data division
>Procedure division

The first division contains descriptive information identifying the program and giving, if necessary, the name of the programmer and the date when it was written. The second division specifies the computer configuration to be used to compile the source program and later to run the object program. The data division specifies files and records and allocates names to them, quoting in detail the contents and format of data records. The procedure division contains the sequence of instructions for processing the data.

FORTRAN

(FORmula TRANslator) is also a universal language, used mainly for programming mathematical problems. It is written in simple English statements, and permits mathematical expressions to be stated naturally in a form of algebraic notation. Since it is not far removed from the language of normal scientific and mathematical usage, it is fairly easily used by the mathematician and scientist without requiring them to be computer experts as well.

ALGOL

(ALGOrithmic Language) was the result of efforts to standardise a large number of algebraic languages used on different machines. It is basically a language for processing mathematical problems. An Algorithm precisely describes a procedure for solving a particular problem. An Algol program consists of a number of statements defining algorithms.

CONSTRUCTING A PROGRAM

Having discussed the different types and levels of computer language, we will now turn our attention to the stages involved in actually constructing a computer program.

Before the programmer starts work on a project there are two things he will require. The first of these is a program specification. This will probably be drawn up by the systems analyst designing the system, and will describe precisely what the program is required to do and include a definition of the files and records that will be used in the procedure. The second is a specification of the computer configuration available to run the program. It will state what input and output devices are available, the amount of available central processor storage, types of backing store and so on. Proceeding then to the preparation of the program, the following stages will be worked through:

(a) Defining the logic of the program.
(b) Recording the logic.
(c) Encoding the program instructions.
(d) Desk checking the instructions.
(e) Preparing the instructions in machine input form.
(f) Compiling the program.
(g) Checking and correcting the compilation i.e. debugging.
(h) Testing the program.
(i) Release for use.

Defining the Logic

This is probably the most difficult part of programming, and the one which entails the greatest amount of creative thinking. The programmer is concerned with working out a logical sequence of operations that will cope with any combination of the variables that the program must deal with to achieve the required result. While there are no standard procedures to induce logical and creative thinking, rough charting at this stage can help the programmer to visualise alternative approaches to the problem, and to construct a picture of the flow of processing procedures. On the principle that two heads are better than one it is often useful to exchange ideas with other programmers, especially those having experience in the particular problems involved.

Recording the Logic

When the sequence of operations making up the program has been mapped out, it should be formally recorded. The most usual way of doing this is to use the conventional programming flowchart with appropriate explanations where necessary. These flowcharts are discussed in more detail in chapter 8. At this stage, a check that the program meets the requirements of the procedure should be made by mentally tracing test data through the flowchart to ensure that the correct results are obtained.

Encoding the Program Instructions

This is the process of translating the program steps indicated on the flowchart into a programming language. Obviously the language used will determine the form of the coding. For this purpose pre-printed programming sheets are usually used. These sheets set out the general format that the program instructions must take.

Desk Checking

The program should now be checked as completely as possible to ensure the accuracy of the encoding. This will prevent the wastage of computer time which will occur later on if transcription errors have not been corrected.

Preparing input

In this stage the coded instructions are prepared in a form suitable for computer input, which is usually in punched tape or punched card form. As an aid to quick and accurate punching, the pre-punched programming sheets mentioned above are ruled so that each line, representing a card, is divided into 80 spaces representing the 80 columns on the card.

Compiling

The process of converting the source program into an object program is known as 'compilation'. As we saw earlier, the compiler is a program in machine language. It is stored in the central processor, and then the source program is read in as data. The instructions in the compiler govern the conversion of the computer language statements of the source program into the machine language instructions of the object program. As each source program instruction is read in, the compiler scans it for errors in construction of the statements.

If any such faultily constructed instructions are found, the compiler will give instructions for them to be printed out for the attention of the programmer. These error messages are known as Diagnostics. In practice the complete source program is often printed out with appropriate notes made against each erroneous statement, and the number of errors shown at the bottom of the page. If the source program is free of errors the compiler produces the object program in machine code.

Debugging

The process of correcting the errors shown in the compilation is known as debugging. Having done this, the compilation routine is repeated until a correct source program is obtained.

Testing the program

The diagnostic errors found in the compiling process are only errors of syntax, that is, errors in the *form* of the instructions. Logical errors in the construction of the program will not be revealed by this process. It is thus quite possible for the program to be formally correct in its use of the programming language, but to be unable to process input data correctly. It is therefore essential to test it, using specimen data of the type it has been designed to process. For this purpose, the object program produced during the final compiling run is read into store and used to process a range of test data specified by the systems analyst. If the correct results are not obtained, amendments will have to be made to the source program. This means that the object program will have to be discarded, and the whole process of compilation carried out again with the revised source program until finally a fully proved object program is produced.

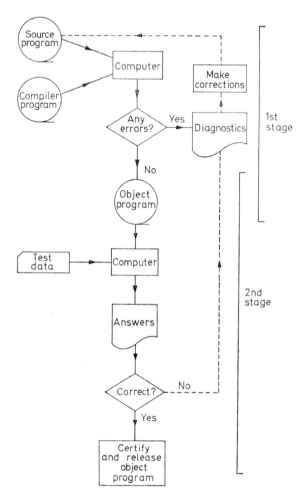

Fig. 11.3—Compiling and Testing a Program

Release for use

The object program output from the computer will have to be stored so that it is available for future use for processing data. It may be punched into cards, written to magnetic tape or to magnetic discs. The general procedure would then be for the chief programmer to certify it as being correct, and pass it over to the library where it would be stored and issued for use as required. (See fig. 11.3.)

SUB-ROUTINES

We have seen that a program is a complete list of instructions for performing a procedure or set of procedures on a computer. Any part of a program dealing with a particular aspect of the program is known as a Routine. For example, checking a customer's order against his credit limit would be a 'routine'. Standard routines that are used repeatedly in a program are known as Sub-routines. In order to save repeating the instructions making up a sub-routine every time it is required in the program, the sub-routine is included once only. Control is transferred to it when required and then back to the main program when it has been executed, entering the program at the instruction immediately following the one calling in the sub-routine. Many standard sub-routines may be obtained from the computer manufacturer for incorporation into programs. The use of sub-routines not only saves programming time but also economises in the use of storage space. An example of the use of a sub-routine is given in fig. 11.4.

Finally it must be mentioned that in a computer processing run the program instructions, or selected groups of instructions as required, will be repeatedly executed for each data item to be processed. For example, if we were processing 1,000 Sales Invoices to up-date a Sales Ledger, then the processing instructions in the program would be run through 1,000 times. This facility, built into the program to direct itself back to an earlier instruction and to repeat a routine, is known as 'looping' and the segment of the program containing the instructions to be repeated as a 'loop'. Naturally some kind of test must be applied to determine whether the set of instructions are to be repeated or not, otherwise the machine would continue to work through them indefinitely. This can be quite a simple program instruction such as 'Is this the end of the file?' Examples of loops can be found in the illustrations in the chapters on Flowcharting and Applications.

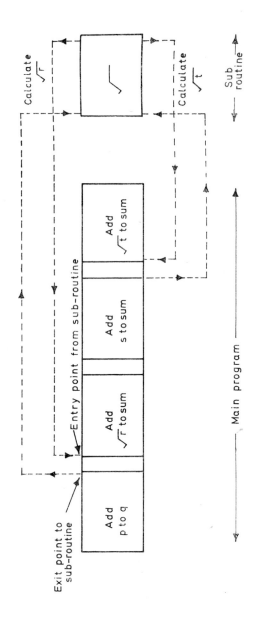

Fig. 11.4—Illustrating the use of a √sub-routine to solve $p+q+\sqrt{r}+s+\sqrt{t}$

EXERCISES CHAPTER 11

1. Explain, preferably with a diagram, the relationship between a sub-routine and the main program and explain how a sub-routine differs from a loop (a detailed flowchart is not required).
   (Royal Society of Arts—Computer Appreciation—Stage II)
2. Explain what is meant by the terms:
   (a) Source Program.
   (b) Object Program.
3. What is the purpose of an Assembler Program. Explain the part this plays in communicating a program to the computer.
4. What are the main stages in preparing a computer program?
5. A program may contain errors in construction and also errors in logic. Distinguish between these two types of error and explain the methods that can be used to trace them.
6. Distinguish between an Assembler Program and a Compiler Program.
7. What do you understand by the term 'High Level Language'? Illustrate your answer by quoting examples of this type of language mentioning the type of problem for which they are normally used.
8. 'A programmer, writing in a high level language, need not have a detailed knowledge of the computer's machine code'.
   Discuss this statement.
9. What do you understand as an 'Instruction Format'. What information would you expect an instruction format to contain?
10. Distinguish between 'Interpreting' and 'Translating' in connection with the use of an Assembler program.
11. Write short notes on
    (a) Diagnostics.
    (b) Debugging.
    (c) Desk Checking.
    (d) Program Testing.
12. What are the stages in writing and documenting a program?
    (Royal Society of Arts—Computer Appreciation—Stage I)

12

Organisation of a Data Processing Department

We have already considered some of the processes that are applied to data in order to achieve the outputs that are called for by the system. The purpose of this chapter is to consider the organisation of the department responsible for carrying out these processes, usually known as a Data Processing Department.

DATA PROCESSING

Perhaps it would be as well to start by trying to define what is meant by Data Processing. We saw earlier that data can be looked on as being a mass of facts and figures that need to be processed in some way to provide meaningful information. The three numbers 70, 30 and 6 in themselves have no value as information, together in a certain sequence they can indicate a date: 30.6.70=30th June 1970.

Data processing then is concerned with the conversion of data into a form suitable for further use according to precise rules of procedure. It is concerned with such techniques as recording, calculating, summarising, classifying and sorting, with the object of providing a useful and meaningful product.

The actual mechanics of processing may take a number of different forms. They can be purely manual or they may make use of some kind of machine. Different types of machines may be used, hand-operated mechanical machines, electro-mechanical machines and electronic machines. Data processing is a comprehensive term used to mean all ways in which data is processed, but in order to distinguish between these ways, the following terms are also often used:

Automatic Data Processing (A.D.P.)

The processing of data by the operation of machines in such a way as to reduce to a minimum the need for manual processing. This term is generally accepted as referring to all types of machine;

accounting machines, calculators, punched card machines as well as computers.

Electronic Data Processing (E.D.P.)

This term is used specifically when data is mainly processed by electronic means and in normal usage it refers to the processing of data by a computer.

Every organisation is involved in processing data in one form or another even if it is only just a question of putting its activities on record. In most business organisations, data processing has a tendency to be departmentalised in the sense that each department is provided with the machines and staff best suited for its particular purpose. A computer is a very versatile machine that can cope with all forms of data processing by using different programs. Thus the computer is able to deal with work done by accounting machines in the finance department, with work done on calculating machines in the invoicing department, with work done manually in the stock control department and so on. Because the computer cuts across departmental boundaries by providing a general processing service, there is a very good argument for data processing to be a department in its own right not subject to the control of any specialist section of the business.

This is the view taken in the following account of the organisation of a Data Processing department although it is recognised that sometimes a machine is installed to do work for just one or two departments and in this case control could well be in the hands of the heads of department concerned.

STRUCTURE OF A DATA PROCESSING DEPARTMENT

While the detailed organisational structure of a D.P. department will depend to a large extent on the size of the organisation it serves and the services it is expected to supply, it will be concerned with the following main areas of work:

1. The investigation of present systems and procedures and the design of systems for computer application.
   This is the work of Systems Analysts.
2. The conversion of the systems specifications provided by the analysts into instructions that can be performed by the computers. This is the work of Programmers.
3. The performance of the operations and procedures within the data processing department. This includes such things as the acceptance and control of data, the preparation of data in a

machine acceptable form, operating the computer and ancillary machines, the control of work flow, file and program usage and so on. This third area of work is the responsibility of the operations manager.

The whole of the department, systems analysts, programmers and operations, is under the control of a Data Processing Manager.

The organisational structure of a department involved in these areas of work could take the form illustrated in fig. 12.1. While a more detailed account is given of some of them in other chapters, the following are comments on the functions involved.

Data Processing Manager

It is evident that many departments of an organisation depend on the Data Processing department for their processing needs. To carry out their function efficiently, they must be able to rely on the reports produced. Because of this, the data processing manager holds a key position in the organisation. He should have the ability to be able to preserve good relationships between his own and the user departments, and have the tact and drive necessary to cope with the problems and difficulties that are bound to arise in these relationships.

In order to efficiently control his highly specialised staff he should have a good practical experience of data processing and a working knowledge of all the activities involved. He must keep up to date with current developments in the computer field and be able to advise management accordingly. He should have an open mind which is not intolerant of new ideas, and be capable of clear, logical and imaginative thinking. The ability to communicate effectively is most important, not only with technicians but with laymen, bearing in mind that he will be dealing with his Board of Directors, the heads of other departments, his own staff and the computer's manufacturer.

System Analysis

As we saw earlier, data processing is a means to an end. Data is raw material consisting to a great extent of a mass of unrelated facts and figures. Processing is the technique of relating all these, and the required end is the provision of meaningful information. The context within which this is all carried out is known as a System, and the system comprises all the detailed rules and procedures which must be observed to give the required end product. By usage, the term 'system' usually applies to a major activity of the business,

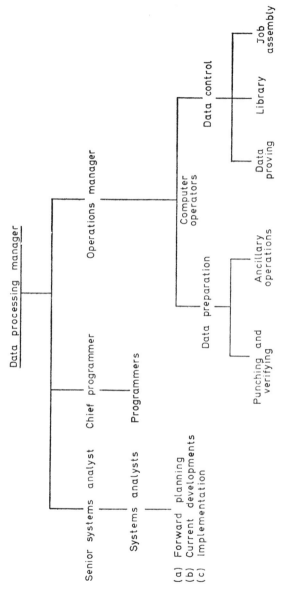

Fig. 12.1—Organisation Chart of a Data Processing Department

for instance, a Sales Ledger System, or a Stock Inventory System. In the latter case we are concerned with relating a mass of data recording stock issues, stock receipts, minimum stock levels, unit prices etc. When processed these will provide up to date statements of current stock levels and values, re-order lists, analysis of material usage and so on.

These systems exist in every business but usually not in a form suitable for processing by computer. The Systems Analyst has as his aim the design of a system that can be so processed. This entails three main functions:

(a) Investigation into, and analysis of existing systems.

(b) The design of systems for computer application to attain pre-determined aims.

(c) The implementation (or putting into action) of the new systems.

The range of work and techniques with which the systems analyst becomes involved is very wide, so he needs a lot of general experience in commercial systems as well as a good knowledge of data processing and computers. He should also have a detailed knowledge of the policy and organisation of the company with which he is working.

As it would be unusual to find any one person with this wide range of experience and knowledge, it is usual for analysts to work in a team. Ideally each member of the team would possess specialist experience in one or more areas of work. The combined 'know-how' of the team can then be brought to bear on the wide range of problems inherent in systems design. The team is usually led by a Senior Systems Analyst who is responsible to the Data Processing Manager.

Success in the investigation and design of a system depends to a large extent on the ability of the systems analyst to enlist the co-operation of members of staff involved who, indeed, may not (for one reason or another) welcome the changes brought about by the introduction of a computer. The analyst must, therefore, be a person able to mix easily with people and to communicate effectively. Other qualities required by an analyst are a capacity for logical thinking, a high standard of accuracy, patience, tact and the ability to record his work clearly and concisely and to work to target dates.

Systems analysts will have three main tasks:

(a) Forward planning, i.e. investigation of systems that are planned for the fairly distant future.

(b) Current development, i.e. the detailed specification of systems planned for implementation in the near future.

(c) Implementation. Supervising the testing and taking over by the computer of systems when design has been completed.

Programming

Programmers usually take over when the analyst has completed the design of a new computer system and has documented the design in the form of a Systems Specification. Basically the program is a series of coded instructions that can be stored in the central processor and executed in the appropriate sequence. Two qualities required of the programmer are the ability to reason logically and to pay very careful attention to detail. The need to document programs with complete accuracy and to conform with recognised standards imposes additional disciplines on the programmer. Systems analysis and programming are discussed in more detail in chapters 10 and 11 respectively.

DATA PROCESSING OPERATIONS

Analysts and programmers are concerned largely with work of a 'once only' nature. They may be responsible from time to time for amendments and alterations to a system, but once it has been designed, documented and programmed, and starts to be used for routine processing operations, it becomes the responsibility of the operations section. While the structural organisation of this section will depend to a great extent on the size of the department and the volume and variety of data processing work, the following basic functions fall within its area of responsibility (see fig. 12.2).

RECORDING-CONVERSION-PROCESSING-REPORTING

Because it provides a service for user departments, the operations section has a continuous two-way flow of work: source data flows in and reports flow out. As well as this, there is a considerable movement of data within the section itself. Source documents go to data preparation, input documents to the computer machine room, output reports from the machine room and so on. Also, the operations section must work to a quite rigid timetable to ensure that reports are available when required, input data is ready for processing when needed and to ensure efficient usage of available machine time. To co-ordinate all of these activities to meet specified deadlines and to ensure the accuracy and security of processing generally, an effective control must be imposed on the work of the operations department. This is usually done by forming a Control section which is responsible for organising the flow of work through the depart-

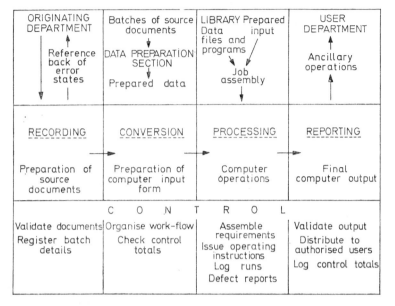

ORIGINATING DEPARTMENT	Batches of source documents	LIBRARY Prepared Data input files and programs	USER DEPARTMENT
Reference back of error states	DATA PREPARATION SECTION	Job assembly	Ancillary operations
	Prepared data		
RECORDING	CONVERSION	PROCESSING	REPORTING
Preparation of source documents	Preparation of computer input form	Computer operations	Final computer output
C O N T R O L			
Validate documents Register batch details	Organise work-flow Check control totals	Assemble requirements Issue operating instructions Log runs Defect reports	Validate output Distribute to authorised users Log control totals

Fig. 12.2—Basic Functions of a Data Processing Department

ment, co-ordinating its activities and imposing standards to ensure the accuracy and security of data processed.

RECORDING

While it is not the responsibility of the data processing department to originate source data, since this is done in the other departments of the organisation, it is the province of the control section to check that data is originated in a way that conforms with procedures laid down when the system was designed and accepted.

As a basic principle, all source data coming into the installation must be handed to a reception clerk. This is the link between the computer and the user departments. The staff of the departments which originate the data should not have unrestricted access to the rest of the computer staff.

Source documents are usually handed in at reception in batches at the frequency and times specified in procedure manuals. Each batch should be accompanied by a Control Slip which gives, where appropriate, an identification of the documents, the number in the batch and their sequence numbers, any control totals obtained by pre-listing and the initials of the person authorised to release the documents for processing. One of the responsibilities of the control section is to check at this point that the documents contained in the batch conform with the details on the control slip and to check as far as possible that they have been accurately completed and are legible. Registers are maintained by the control section in which batch details (date, sequence numbers and any control totals) are recorded.

So that queries may be quickly resolved, there should be a defined procedure for reference back to the originating department of any question arising when checking source documents. The aim should be to ensure that source data is correct before it is passed on from reception to the data preparation section, since the sooner an error is detected, the less trouble is caused in correcting it.

While the principle of batching source documents is discussed in detail in chapter 9, the following advantage of this procedure are mentioned in connection with data preparation:

(a) It presents punch operators with reasonable sized jobs.
(b) It facilitates the tracing of errors. The reason for failure to reconcile control totals is more easily found if the error occurs in a fairly small batch.
(c) It allows errors to be traced in one batch while processing continues with those batches that have been proved correct.

CONVERSION

We have already seen that it is usually necessary to convert source data to an input form suitable for machines. This is known as Data Preparation and is the work of the Data Preparation section of the data processing department. This section contains the machines for converting source data (usually punched card or punched paper tape machines) and operators who are under the control of a Punch Room Supervision. The control section is responsible for the flow of work through the data preparation stage, to ensure that prepared data is available in time for scheduled computer runs. Batches of source documents are handed to the supervisor who allocates work to the operators and supervises the punching and verifying. Punch operators must be supplied with clear written instructions for the preparation of each card form and a specimen of the card format. Other than punching and verifying, the data preparation section may be involved with the extraction of control totals by passing cards through a punched card tabulator and with using punched card sorters to put the cards in a required sequence.

Once they have been punched and verified, source documents should be cancelled, to prevent their re-entry into the system. This is often done by requiring operators to stamp source documents with a numbered rubber stamp. This serves the purposes both of cancelling the source document and of identifying the operator who punched the data from it.

Control totals taken from the prepared data are compared by the control section with the totals previously noted from the source documents control slip. This process of comparison of totals helps to detect errors made in the data preparation section.

The general process of controlling the accuracy of punching and verifying, the correction of errors and reconciliation of totals is usually known as Data Proving. (See fig. 12.3.)

PROCESSING

Before a processing run takes place, the computer operators must be supplied with all the materials necessary for the run. Getting all these requirements together, another function of the control section, is known as Job Assembly. It is usual to specify the requirements for individual runs in the procedure manuals prepared when the system was first designed. While, of course, these will vary with the type of run, the following is a typical list:

(a)   Operating instructions stating exactly what processing is to take place.
(b)   The program necessary for the run.
(c)   The job input data.
(d)   Any pre-printed stationery for output.
(e)   Any files required. Assuming magnetic tape files are used, this would include any Master Files for up-dating and any tapes for taking on the results of processing. These latter may be completely blank tapes, or tapes containing data no longer required that can now be over-written.

Staffing arrangements for the computer room will depend on the size of the installation and on work volumes, but will consist basically of a Computer Room Supervisor and a number of operators. As it is desirable to run computers for as many hours a day as possible, shift working may often be involved, with a number of operating teams each under the control of a shift leader.

Operators are expected to keep a 'log' recording the utilisation of the machine time and to report any defects resulting in the loss of machine time, whether these arise through mechanical failures or defects in input data or programs.

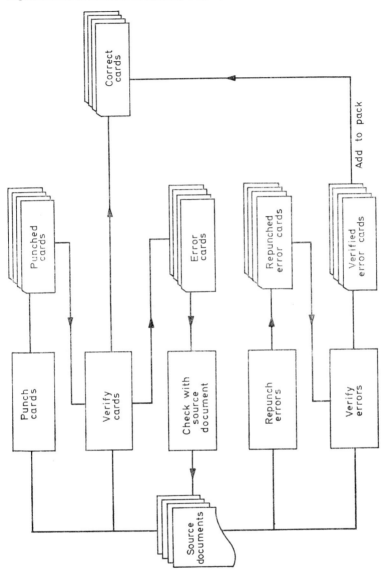

Fig. 12.3—Routine for preparation of Punched Cards from Source
Documents

C.A.—G*

One function vitally important to smooth processing is the control of the storage and use of data files and programs. A large installation could well be concerned with the storage and use of hundreds of magnetic tapes. These contain programs and master data representing the information requirements not only of the processing department but of the whole organisation. It is essential, therefore, that suitable physical conditions are available for maintaining the tapes in good order and that controls are imposed to ensure the use of the correct tapes in processing and the security of the information they contain. The section of the department responsible for this is known as a Tape Library, and is under the control of a Librarian.

The conditions necessary for storing magnetic tapes are basically those required in the computer room itself. These are discussed in chapter 12. For this reason it is often convenient for the library to be situated in a section of the computer machine room that has been fitted with storage racks on which the tapes, in their individual dust-proof containers, can be stored.

The control of the use of tapes centres around the upkeep of records designed to identify the contents of each tape and to record their issue to and receipt from the machine room. Notes must also be kept on the physical condition of each tape. Most important, a note must be kept of the date until which recorded data must be preserved. This is known as a 'Purge Date', and on or after the purge date the tape can be over-written with new data.

REPORTING

Another of the functions of the control section is to accept output reports from the computer machine room and arrange for their distribution to the departments authorised to receive them. Before distribution the validity of the report should be checked against the format specified in procedure manuals and any control totals noted in the appropriate register. In addition to this, ancillary machine operations may be called for such as bursting continuous stationery, collating, folding and so on. A description of these ancillary operations is given in the chapter on Output.

Finally, in relation to the general organisation of a Data Processing department, the following points should be noted:

1. Staff duties should be clearly defined in writing and an organisation chart prepared for the department.

2. The organisation should be arranged to guard against the possibility of the whole department grinding to a halt through the absence or irregular conduct of one member of staff.
3. Allowance must be made for the observance of any legal requirements, such as auditing, and also for any special constraints imposed by management.
4. Computer department staff should not be allowed to take part in the preparation of source documents or, other than the control and data preparation staff, have access to them.
5. For security purposes the various sections of the department should, as far as possible, be physically separated, access to the records controlled by each section being strictly limited to those people responsible for them.
6. Strict control must be imposed over important documents, such as blank cheque forms and wage payment slips.
7. Access to the computer machine room and to the library files should be strictly limited.
8. The general aims of the control section of the department are:
   (a) To organise the flow of work through the department as smoothly and efficiently as possible.
   (b) To conform with the times set for the production of output reports.
   (c) To ensure as far as possible the detection and correction of errors thus saving time and money otherwise wasted in re-processing.
   (d) To keep the records and to ensure the procedures that satisfy legal and auditing requirements.
   (e) To prevent any deliberate mal-practices.

EXERCISES CHAPTER 12

1. Outline the main functions of the Control section of a Data Processing department.
2. Differentiate between Data Processing, Automatic Data Processing and Electronic Data Processing.
3. What main sections would you expect to find in a D.P. department? Give a short account of the work of each.
4. Describe the flow of any processing job of your choice through a data processing department from the time the source documents are handed in at reception until the distribution of the final reports.

5. What qualities would you look for in a person applying for the position of Data Processing Manager?
6. Describe the work of the Data Preparation Section of a D.P. department.
7. What do you understand by the term 'Job Assembly'? Illustrate your answer by relating it to a computer run to up-date a Sales Ledger file by movement data.
8. Outline the duties of a Librarian in an installation using magnetic tape storage.
9. What are the duties and responsibilities of three of the following:
   (a) Systems Analyst
   (b) Tape Librarian
   (c) Programmers
   (d) Punch Machine Operators
   (e) Computer Operators.
   (Royal Society of Arts—Computer Appreciation—Stage I)
10. (a) Show diagrammatically the structure of that part of a typical data processing department which is the responsibility of the operations manager.
    (b) Indicate the functions of each section shown in your answer to (a) by describing briefly the events which occur between a user department submitting data to the computer department and receiving their results.
    (Institute of Data Processing)

13

Applications

In this chapter a number of computer applications are described These have been deliberately kept fairly simple, since the object is to illustrate the type of work that is commonly the subject of electronic processing and to demonstrate some of the techniques and devices described in this book. The descriptions of these applications are not intended to represent complete systems definitions.

If we start by considering one main business function, that of Sales, we find that in dealing with and in recording a credit sale to a customer the following main areas of work are involved:

(a) Receipt of customer's order.

(b) Vetting for credit control purposes, with procedures for opening new accounts where appropriate.

(c) Preparing the documents relating to the transaction: Stores despatch instructions, Advice Note, Invoice etc.

(d) Calculating the price of the goods sold.

(e) Packing and dispatching the goods.

(f) Up-dating stores inventory.

(g) Up-dating Sales Ledger and preparation of customer Sales Statements.

(h) Sales Analysis.

Now the range of work within this main function, Sales, that is performed by computer will vary from situation to situation. For instance, the entry point for computer processing could be at (b) which means that the credit control procedures, preparation of documents, stock inventory, sales ledger and sales analysis would all be performed by the machine. On the other hand perhaps all the stages up to and including the preparation of the invoice are manual procedures and the entry point for the computer is at (f) Stock Inventory.

From this series of procedures it is proposed to select just two routines. The first assumes the entry point to computer processing to be a manually completed invoice, and is just concerned with up-dating a Sales Ledger and the production of a Sales Analysis. The second assumes the entry point to be a completed Advice Note and is only concerned with up-dating a Stock Inventory and the production of invoices for distribution to customers.

SALES LEDGER APPLICATION

The first routine is described below and also shown in chart form in fig. 13.1 (a), (b) and (c).

The output requirements are:

(a) Monthly Sales Ledger accounts and Customers' Sales Statements. These will contain the balance outstanding at the start of the month, a list of the movements during the month in date order, and finally the balance outstanding at the end of the month.

(b) Sales Analysis over sales areas.

Records that need to be kept on file to produce these outputs are:

(i) Master Records. Each record containing the customer's name and address, customer account reference number, balance on the account and the date of the balance. In order to provide an area sales analysis, the first digit of the account number is the key to the sales area.

(ii) Movement Records. These record all movement items, details of sales being obtained from invoices, returns and allowances from credit notes, cash received and discounts from cash books and so on.

(iii) Change Records. These are needed for opening new accounts, deleting from file accounts that have been closed and making amendments such as of address, to customer details.

Master records are held in account number sequence on Magnetic Tape files. Movement data and Changes are prepared on Punched Cards from batches of source documents received daily at the D.P. Department. Since, in this application, we are only considering the Sales Ledger and Analysis over areas, we are not interested in the individual items on the invoice as we would be for a Stock Inventory up-dating.

For each movement item a card will be prepared containing the customer account number, the date, a code to indicate the type of

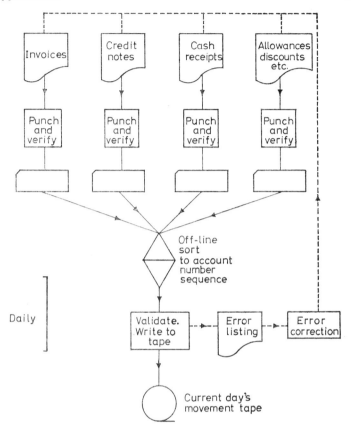

Fig. 13.1 (a)—Preparation of 'Movements' File in a Sales Ledger Application

transaction—invoice, credit note, cash etc.—and the amount. Cards recording changes will have to be designed to include full customer details, name, address, account number, to provide the information to open a new account on the master file. The batches of source documents will be pre-listed and control totals obtained before punching and these in turn will be checked against totals obtained from the batches of cards after completion of the punching operation.

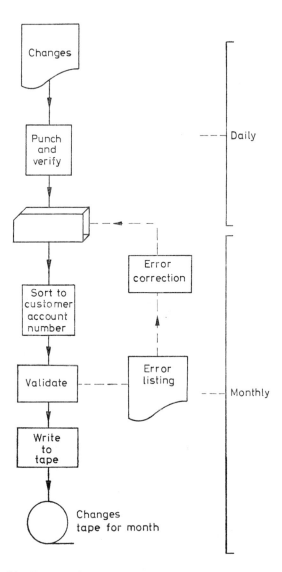

Fig. 13.1 (b)—Preparation of 'Changes' File in a Sales Ledger Application

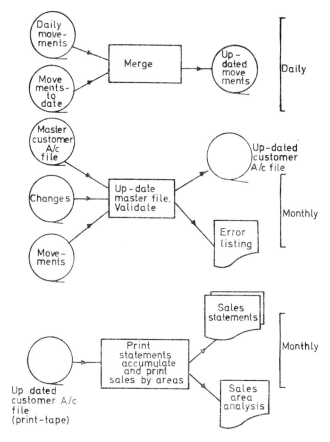

Fig. 13.1 (c)—Computer Runs in a Sales Ledger Application

We now have available, prepared daily, the movement data and the changes in machine input form. Now a number of ways suggest themselves by which the up-dating of the master file can be accomplished from these, bearing in mind that what we are aiming at is a file or files containing the master data and opening balances, and the movement data in date order within account number. Cards could be sorted daily on a Punched Card Sorter and then used as a direct input to up-date the master file each day. They could be assembled over a week or even a month and then sorted mechanically and then used to up-date the master file.

Another way would be to write them in random order to magnetic tape and then sort them on the tape to the required sequence, using this sorted movements tape to up-date the master file. All these represent possible ways in which the problem could be tackled and the method chosen will depend on such things as volumes of data, available hardware and the amount of computer time available.

For the purpose of this example we will assume that the daily output of movement cards is mechanically sorted into customer account number sequence. The cards are then written to a magnetic tape that we will call a Movements tape. The cards recording changes, since these will be fairly few in number, will be kept on a punched card file for processing at the end of the month.

Each subsequent day's movement is applied to the movements file in a daily up-dating run on the computer. This means that at the end of the month we have a file containing all the movements in date order within account number. Next the monthly changes cards are sorted mechanically and written to a further magnetic tape. This now leaves us with three tape files, the master file containing opening balances, a movement file and a changes file. The next procedure is to process these three tapes on the computer to merge all the data they contain on to a fourth tape. This we can call a 'Print' tape, which will in turn be used to print out the information we require. During the preparation of the print tape any errors, for example, movement items for account numbers not appearing on either the master or changes files, will be printed out so that a manual check can be made.

The final stage, then, is to run the print tape to produce on a line printer the Sales Ledger Accounts and the Customer Statement. At the same time, customer master data and closing balances are written to another tape, this becoming the opening master tape for the next accounting period.

While the records are being processed and printing is taking place, the value of those records carrying a code indicating 'Sales' are accumulated in store locations according to the first digit in the account number indicating the Sales area. At the end of the run the totals in these locations are printed out to provide the Sales Analysis.

STOCK INVENTORY APPLICATION

In the second case, this is shown in chart form in fig. 13.2, we are considering a simple application involving a Stock Inventory up-dating procedure and the preparation of Sales Invoices for distribution to customers. The entry point to computer processing is, in this case, the Advice Note prepared manually when the goods are despatched.

The output requirements are:
(a) An up-dated Stock Inventory.
(b) A list of stock items to be re-ordered.
(c) An analysis of sales under product groups.
(d) Customer invoices.

We will assume again that files are held on magnetic tape and that input data is prepared on punched cards. A master record is held on file for each stock item. This contains the item part number and description, unit price, re-order level, current stock level and current stock value. There is also a magnetic tape file containing master records for customers including customer account number, name and address. Data records on both of these files are arranged in key number sequence, that is part number sequence or customer account number sequence.

The main processing requirements of the procedures are:

(a) To price and to calculate the value of each item appearing on the advice notes. This means multiplying the unit price by the quantity.

(b) To apply these quantities and values to up-date the master stock record file.

(c) To compare stock levels after up-dating with re-order levels and to print out a list of stock items where re-order level is equal to or greater than current stock.

(d) To print customer invoices containing customer name and address, date, a list of items supplied as shown on the advice note each with the quantity, unit price and value, and the invoice total.

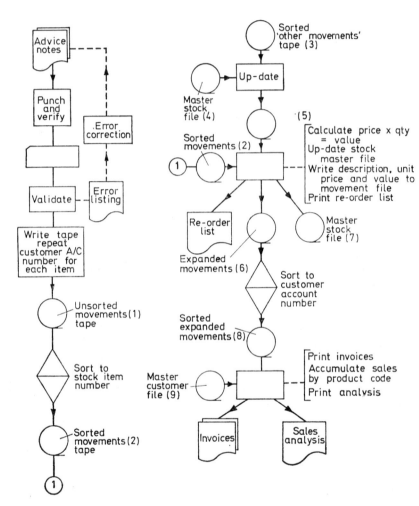

Fig. 13.2—Stock Inventory, Sales Invoices and Sales Analysis

(e) To print an analysis of sales under stock product groups, this group being indicated by the first two digits in the stock item number.

The main problem in this kind of application where master records are held in sequence on tape, is that the movement data has to be arranged in a different sequence for different purposes. That is, for stock inventory up-dating the movement records must be in stock item number order, and for preparing the invoices the records must be in customer account number order. This means that, as stock items must be priced and extended before the invoice is prepared, they must be sorted into stock item number sequence but still not lose their identity in relation to the customer to whom the goods have been sold.

The following set of procedures is just one suggested routine to achieve the output objectives listed earlier:

1. The preparation of punched cards from the advice notes. These cards must identify the customer and record the items of stock and quantities sold. For this purpose we will use a 'Spread Card' (this has been described in the chapter on Inputs), containing a code to identify the type of transaction, the date, customer account number and then, across the card under stock item number and quantity headings, details of the goods supplied.

2. The records on these cards are then written to a magnetic tape, which we will call a Movement Tape (1). In doing so the customer account number is repeated for each individual stock item. Thus, while the original record appeared on the card as:

Customer A/c number	Stock Item number	Qty.	Stock Item number	Qty.	Stock Item number	Qty.
12345	2469	24	1369	50	8642	32

On the magnetic tape it will appear as:

    12345 2469 24 : 12345 1369 50 : 12345 8642 32

In doing this each individual stock item is identified with the customer. An alternative way is to relate each stock item to the advice note number on which it appears and to keep a file indexing advice note numbers to customer account numbers. This latter method could well be preferable if a number of customer orders are in the same batch and it is required to prepare a separate invoice for each.

3. Next the movements tape is sorted into stock item number sequence (2).

4. In the meantime details of other stock movements, goods received, returns to store etc., and any additions, deletions and amendments to master records have been prepared on cards and in turn written to magnetic tape (3) and sorted into stock item number sequence.

5. Assuming at this point only four tape decks to be available, the next procedure would be to run the other stock movements tape (3) against the master stock tape (4) to produce another master tape up-dated by stock receipts and amendments (5).

6. The movements tape (2) is now processed with the up-dated master tape (5). In this run, having located the correct stock item master record by comparison of stock item numbers, the description and unit price is copied from the master to the movement record, a calculation made—quantity in movement record times unit price—and the resultant value added to the movement record. The original data in the record on the movement tape plus the data copied from the master record plus the results of the calculation are written to a third tape which we will call the Expanded Movements Tape. (6) The record on this will now appear as:

Customer A/c number	Stock Item number	Stock Item Description	Quantity	Unit Price	Value

In the meantime the records on the master tape are themselves up-dated by the movements, new balances created and the up-dated records written to a fourth tape which becomes an up-dated master tape (7). During this process, the revised balance is compared with the re-order level and if it is not greater, a print-out is made, identifying the stock item and showing the current stock and the re-order level. This means we have now accomplished the first two objectives, an up-dated stock inventory file and the preparation of a re-order list.

7. The expanded movements tape (6), at present containing records in stock item number sequence, must now be sorted back to customer account number sequence (8), thus re-assembling the stock items as they first appeared on the advice note. However, the customer is still only identified by the customer account number. For the purpose of printing the invoice we need the customer name and address.

8. These names and addresses are contained in the records on the master customer file (9) and by running this with the expanded

movements tape (8) either a print tape can be written from which invoices can be printed at a later time, or the invoices printed direct at this stage. During this run, sales analysed under product group indicated by the first two digits in the stock item number, can be accumulated in store for printing out at the end of the run.

The two applications described so far are just basic routine clerical jobs performed by computer. They do not involve the use of one of the computer's more powerful facilities, that is the direct interrogation of records to obtain data at very short notice. This, as we saw earlier in the chapter on Storage, is not practical in a configuration using files that can be only serially accessed, but involves the use of direct access file devices such as Magnetic Drums or Discs, from which data can be extracted at random.

PRODUCTION CONTROL

Let us move on now from applications in purely commercial data processing. A significant proportion of the computers used in this country, probably amounting within a short time to one-sixth of the total, are used in production control. It is apparent that very great benefits can arise from the use of computers to ensure the optimum utilisation of production resources. If we say that production control techniques have as their aim the completion of specified work at the right time with the greatest economy in the use of resources, we can see that it might be impossible, using a manual system of control to achieve all these aims at the same time. For example, delays in production might be insured against by carrying over-large stocks of components, thus achieving production at the right time but at the expense of the economical use of resources.

In large scale production so many variables are involved, (work priority, availability of stock, utilisation of available machines and man power, and so on) that reliance on human skill and experience to make all the information on these variables available, to take it all into consideration and to reach the best decision every time is asking the impossible. The computer comes into its own in this field not only by its capacity to store the mass of statistical data involved in production and to make this available in the required form very quickly, but more important by its capacity to weigh up a situation and arrive at a decision. This decision, moreover can take into account all the information the computer has on all the variables and is based on a review of every combination of these variables.

In production control, the first area to feel the impact of computer methods is usually that of Stock Control. By this we mean not merely a convenient mechanism for recording issues and receipts, in other words keeping a Stock Ledger, but the control of stock quantities at their optimum level. This means taking into consideration such things as market trends with seasonal fluctuations in the demand for finished goods, future production requirements for raw materials, the cost of tying up capital in stocks, the cost of storage and the cost of being out of stock, the reliability of suppliers, the necessary re-order time and so on. For a firm keeping thousands of stock items, to manually apply each of these variables to each item of stock would, of course, be an immense task. Given the criteria on which to judge these factors, to the computer the setting of optimum stock levels to meet the conditions prevailing presents no major difficulty.

The computer having determined what stocks are required, its next area of concern is in planning and controlling the production processes necessary to make these stocks available. Usually, in large scale production, the product progresses through a number of production levels. For example, raw materials become component parts, components become sub-assemblies, sub-assemblies become major assemblies which then make up the finished product. The output at each level can be regarded as the 'stock' for the input to the next level. Two main problems arise here:

(a) the maintenance of the correct stock quantities at each production level to provide a continuous work flow, and

(b) the allocation of resources to meet the production requirements at each level. We have already seen earlier, that control of this first factor, stock quantities, can be successfully performed by the computer.

The second factor involves the 'break-down' or analysis of finished products into the requirements at different production levels. This means that the computer must keep on file a record of the components, assemblies etc., that make up each standard finished product. By a process of analysing the make-up of each product, relating this to demand and to already existing stocks, the computer is able to produce a production schedule. In producing this, another factor the machine is able to take into consideration is that of components and assemblies common to two or more finished products so that these can be batch produced to ensure economic production quantities.

The third major area of work the computer is concerned with

is that of scheduling production and allocating resources. We saw earlier that one of the aims in production control is to achieve the greatest economy in the use of resources. One of the most difficult problems in scheduling production on a multi-level basis is to ensure the full utilisation of resources at all levels. A bottleneck at one level of production could well lead to the use of resources at subsequent levels at less than their full capacity. Again, the computer is able to take all the variables into consideration and to schedule production in the most efficient manner. Having implemented the production schedule, there remains the task of comparing performance with plans. This monitoring can be done through the computer by feeding back to it data recording performance. For the information of management, the computer will then report on any failure to meet planned requirements.

Finally, in a fully integrated computer production control system, the effects of changes in scheduled production can be quickly assessed. In a manually controlled system, the effects of a management decision to squeeze in an urgent job are often virtually impossible to assess. However, with computer control, these effects can be quickly and accurately foreseen thus providing the information management needs to make its decisions in a rational and calculated way.

RATES ACCOUNTING

One of the earlier computer applications in this country was in Public Administration for the processing of Rate accounts. In fact a large number of local authorities have now changed, or are in the process of changing over to computer methods for this purpose. While the detail varies from authority to authority, the basic requirements of a rating system are as follows; it must be able to:
1. Maintain an up to date file of records of properties.
2. Periodically calculate the rates due in respect of each property.
3. Prepare and circulate Rate Notices.
4. Keep personal accounts recording amounts due and amounts paid.
5. Record receipts of cash.
6. Periodically list outstanding balances.
7. Prepare Reminder Notices as appropriate.

Initially a Master Rate File is prepared, usually in two sections. The first section contains records of all properties within the rating area, and the second, records of those properties where the owner, rather than the occupier, is the ratepayer. We will assume that these records are held on magnetic tape in property reference number sequence and that the first type of record contains the following information:

(a) Property Reference Number. This is usually based on the geographical location of the property and refers to the District, Street and number within the street.

(b) The basis of the rate assessment—Net Annual Value and Rateable Value—with records of any revision of these.

(c) Occupier's name and address.

(d) A code number to distinguish successive occupiers.

(e) Dates of commencement and/or termination of occupation.

(f) Owner's reference if occupier is not the rate-payer.

(g) Coding to indicate the type of property.

(h) Occupier's personal account showing amounts due and recording cash received.

The second type of record, the Owner's record, contains much the same information, but the sequence key is the Owner's reference rather than the property reference. Since one owner may be responsible for the rates levied on a number of premises, the record may contain a schedule of premises. However, it is more usual in computer processing for a multiple number of records to be held for one owner, each containing details of one property. In either case, the record will identify the property by the property reference number and address, identify the owner by the owner's reference, name and address and will also include details of the rates assessed and the owner's personal account.

With this master rate file as our starting point, the following is a brief description of the processing necessary to achieve the requirements listed earlier. These are shown diagrammatically in figure 13.3 (a) to (f).

1. The revision of the master rate file by changes, e.g. change in basis of assessment, in owner or occupier, addition of new premises or deletion of demolished premises etc. Changes are punched into cards, written to magnetic tape, sorted into key number sequence and applied to amend the master rate file, resulting in Master Rate File (2).

2. Calculation of rates due and preparation of Rates Notices for distribution. In this case the declared rate in the £1 for the various categories of property are read into store from punched cards (the number of rates being very limited). Codings are matched with the property code in the master record on Master Rate File (2) and the rateable value multiplied by the rate in

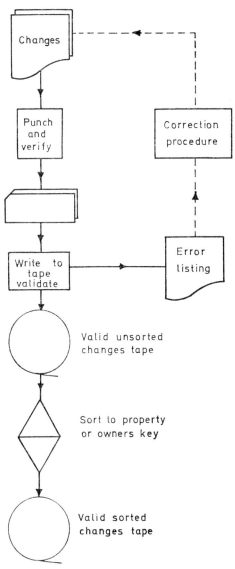

Fig. 13.3 (a)—Treatment of 'changes' in a Rates Application

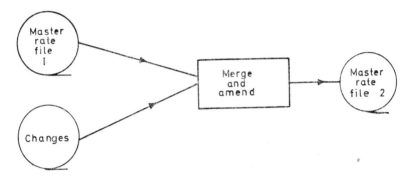

Fig. 13.3 (b)—Amending Master Rates File with Changes

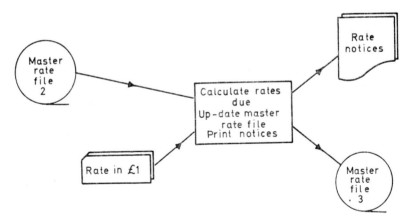

Fig. 13.3 (c)—Calculating Rates due and printing Rates Notices

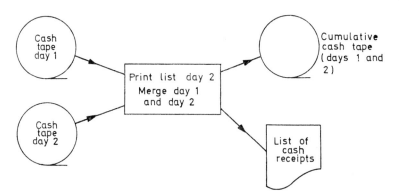

Fig. 13.3 (d)—Treatment of daily cash receipts

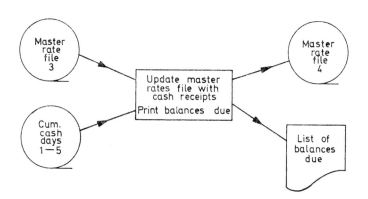

Fig. 13.3 (e)—Posting cash receipts for the week and producing list of balances

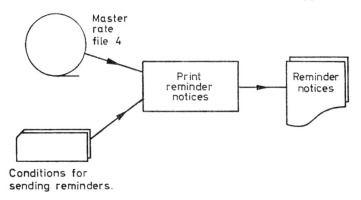

Fig. 13.3 (f)—Printing Reminder Notices

the £1 to calculate the rates due. The Rates Notices are printed and at the same time the rates due written to the record in the Master File, producing an up-dated Master Rates File (3).

3. Next we deal with cash receipts. We will assume the treatment of these will require a daily printed list of cash received and a weekly run to up-date the Master Rates File with the accumulated receipts for the week. To this end, cards are punched daily to record the amount received and the property or owners reference number. These cards are in turn written to magnetic tape and sorted into key sequence. This tape is than used in a print run to prepare the required listing for the first day of the week. A similar tape is prepared for the second day and used to print the second day's receipts, and at the same time the records are merged with the first day so as to produce a cumulative tape containing the first two days' records in sequence. This process is repeated for days 3, 4 and 5 thereby producing at the end of the week, a tape containing records of the receipts for the whole week.

4. This cumulative cash receipts tape is now run with the Master Rates File (3) up-dating the appropriate records and producing a new Master Rates File (4). At the same time a list of the balances due at this stage is printed.

5. The final stage is the preparation of reminder notices. In this case the specified conditions in which reminder notes are to be sent may be written into the program or, on the other hand, be prepared on cards for each individual run. Assuming the latter

to be the case the conditions are read into store where the records from the master tape are compared with them and where appropriate, a reminder notice printed.

EXERCISES CHAPTER 13

1. A Stock File held on magnetic tape contains a sequence of records in ascending order of commodity key. Each week details of receipts and issues are punched into cards. Records on the Stock File are up-dated weekly and it is required to produce an analysis of receipts and issues by product group and also the total value of the stock after up-dating. Draw a flowchart to illustrate these procedures.
2. Describe a routine for producing customer invoices by computer assuming the following to be available:
    (a) Advice Notes containing customer name, address and account number, and a list of the items supplied quoting stock item number and quantity.
    (b) A magnetic tape file of stock records in item number sequence, each record containing item number, description and unit price.
    (c) Assume a central processor, card reader, line printer and four magnetic tape decks to be available.
3. Describe a routine for dealing with (2) above but to cope with three categories of customer A, B and C who are given 15 per cent, 25 per cent and $33\frac{1}{3}$ per cent Trade Discount respectively.
4. Using any computer configuration of your choice describe a routine for dealing with student enrolment in a college in order to produce:
    (a) Lists of students on each course in alphabetical order.
    (b) List of students with two or more 'A' level passes in alphabetical order.
    (c) The average age of students on each course.
5. Give a short account of the advantages that you would expect to be realised in introducing a computer production control system.
6. Describe in outline the uses of the computer in any specialised field with which you are familiar such as modern medical science or Traffic engineering.

(Royal Society of Arts—Computer Appreciation—Stage II)

14

Management

'Going computer' has far reaching effects on an organisation. It is not just the buying of another accounting or calculating machine to fit in neatly with established procedures, but rather the introduction of a key factor around which the whole administrative machinery could well revolve and, upon which it may well depend. Only the highest level of management will be able to authorise the financial outlay, re-definition of responsibilities, and the structural re-organisation necessary to use a computer to the full. It is, therefore, imperative to the success of a computer project that management at director level should be actively involved. This chapter is concerned with the part played by management in relation to the use of computers in an organisation. This will be considered under two main headings, Management Policy and Management Problems.

MANAGEMENT POLICY

The immediate difficulty that faces management in connection with a change-over to computers is that on the one hand they must make decisions, while on the other they cannot be expected to have the necessary expert knowledge. With this in mind we shall look at the complete computer project in three stages. First the situations that suggest installation of a computer, then the initial investigation or feasibility study, and finally the installation of the machine and the implementation of systems.

Later on we will give more detailed consideration to the circumstances which may make the installation of a computer desirable, but the first essential is to decide whether it is worth incurring the cost of a feasibility study. Management should therefore, even at this early stage, have some idea of what a computer can and what it cannot do. The feasibility study is usually conducted by experts, either from independent consultants or from a manufacturer. It is their responsibility to advise management on the desirability of using a machine, to recommend the areas of work that should be taken on and to specify the configuration of the installation needed.

Management should be in a position to make a critical appraisal of the report by having a good idea of what they require from the installation and, as far as possible, some idea of the capabilities of computers. As far as the third stage is concerned, for this management will have appointed their own expert staff, Computer manager, Systems Analysts etc. From this point onwards, active participation of management at director level is again necessary to provide the authority for implementing the changes that must be made. One workable approach to this is to give a director who is not involved in any one particular department of the business, overall responsibility for computer services.

At this point it would be as well to examine the position of the manager of a computer installation. It is impractical to make him responsible to the head of any particular section of the business, because, as we have seen, the effective installation of a computer requires decisions to be made which will affect the working of several departments. In the interests of the business as a whole, these decisions must not be subject to veto or modification by the head of any one department. The computer manager must therefore be directly responsible to the director responsible for computer services. As far as the mechanics of director participation are concerned, a logical solution would be control through a committee with the director as chairman and as members, the computer manager, a representative of the manufacturers supplying the machine and the departmental managers who are, from time to time, directly affected by the planning. While the computer manager would have responsibility for the detailed organisation of his own department and the take-on of the areas of work as these are decided by the committee, the committee should make decisions affecting areas of work outside the computer department and be concerned with overall planning. Another important function of the committee would be to review periodically the progress of the project as reported by the computer manager.

Having emphasised the need for the involvement of management at director level, while the expert technical know-how of the manufacturers and the computer manager cannot be expected of the director concerned, management should not be completely dependent on the experts. The director concerned should make a point of learning all that he can on the subject so that he is able to bring a degree of discernment and critical appraisal to bear on the proposals formulated by the experts. There are a number of ways of going about this of which, perhaps, the two most useful are by attending

C.A.—H

courses put on by manufacturers for executives at this level and by visiting other firms who have installed computers in similar circumstances to find out what their problems have been.

Having discussed the need for management participation in a computer project we should now examine in greater detail the factors that may give rise to consideration of a computer installation. Where does a computer fit in to an organisation?

Since the introduction of computers, not much more than 20 years ago, the general approach to their use has gone through three stages. Initially the computer was designed as a specialist tool for solving a particular problem. The first machines were built to solve problems in aeronautics and ballistics. The realisation that a computer could be used to process routine jobs very quickly led to the second approach, sometimes known as a 'hardware' approach which regarded it as just another machine to perform existing clerical procedures. The attitude during this phase was that the machine should fit into the existing systems environment by taking over the routine repetitive-work done mainly by junior clerks. The third, sometimes known as the 'Systems Approach' takes a far wider view. It looks on the computer as a management tool, involved in decision making formerly performed by middle management, and providing the information to guide policy decisions. In fact it becomes the 'peg' for the re-structuring of the organisation. To some extent, the attitude that a computer is just another grey box to tuck away in the corner of the accounts office still exists, although this is soon dissipated when an investigation into its use starts. In order to get the greatest benefit from the considerable expense involved, management policy must look towards the realisation of the full potential of the machine.

Initial Thinking

We have already considered under the heading of Feasibility Study in chapter 10, the detailed considerations that management will take into account in reaching a decision, but what factors prompt thinking in terms of computers in the first place? It is suggested that the following four motives play their part.

(a) To resolve a problem situation.
(b) To generally increase performance and profitability of the organisation.
(c) To provide a base for re-organisation.
(d) Prestige.

While it was suggested previously that an early and very limited approach to computer use was for solving specific problems, never the less, the existence of a problem situation is a valid reason for thinking in terms of a computer providing that the potentialities of its wider use are also considered. While it is impractical to itemise all the problems that arise in a business, situations do arise which just cannot be coped with by existing resources and methods, due to such things as complexity of work, shortage of trained staff, or increase in work volume.

A firm with such a problem should of course investigate all possible solutions, of which a computer installation is only one, but it may turn out to be the most promising one.

The second situation arises, not so much from a specific problem, but from conditions which make it apparent that the general use of resources, processing methods and control techniques are such that the organisation is not producing either the performance or the profit it could. Investigation into the use of a computer to generally 'tone-up' business activity is again, a sound enough proposition.

The situation we have in mind in the third case is the one in which organisational structure of a business has 'just grown' with the firm's development. This frequently results in recognition at some point that the whole structure is far too complex and top-heavy. Not only is the introduction of a computer a valid reason for carrying out a complete re-organisation but it will also have the effect of streamlining and simplifying processing methods.

Finally, to be realistic, it must be realised that the day is still not past when computers are installed mainly for prestige purposes. It has been said that 40 per cent of the machines used in the U.S.A. were bought mainly from motives of prestige. To the directors concerned this is doubtless a valid reason, but it is doubtful if, under these circumstances, the best is got out of the machine.

Buy, Rent or Bureau?

Management, having decided to adopt computer methods are now faced with a choice between three ways of going about it: (a) to purchase a machine outright from the manufacturer (b) to rent from a manufacturer or (c) to enlist the services of a computer bureau to process the work they have in mind.

Thinking of a computer bureau first, the decision will mainly revolve around the prices charged and the volume of work involved. For a computer to earn its keep it has to put in a lot of hours a day; in fact many installations work round the clock. Obviously, if the volume of work will only be sufficient to keep the machine occupied for a few hours a week, the use of a computer bureau is probably the best approach. It must be remembered that apart from the cost of the machine the cost of creating a computer department can be very high. The provision of accommodation, staff, salaries, systems development cost and the cost of ancillary equipment all have to be taken into consideration. Although when buying time from a computer bureau, a degree of re-organisation and staff retraining is still necessary, the other main items of cost are not directly incurred. Most bureaux, in addition to offering a processing service, will investigate and design the systems required by their clients. At the moment most bureaux work on a basis of receiving source data from clients, processing it and sending back the reports. The current development in this field by forward looking bureaux is to provide a direct access data transmission service by locating input and output peripherals at the client's premises. The client then has direct access to the machine during the time allocated by the bureau. Cost of hiring computer time will, of course, depend on the power of the machine operated by the bureau. It is usually not less than £50 an hour and for really fast and powerful machines may well be more than this.

As far as a decision to rent or buy a machine is concerned, this again is largely a question of balance between economics and volumes of work but a third factor, technical development, should be considered here. Because of the very rapid developments in technical performance of machines, many firms have in the past been reluctant to purchase one outright, taking the view that it was better to hire one and change it when technical advances made this desirable. This argument has not quite so much force now, as to a great extent design seems to have settled down and it is difficult to see any very revolutionary technical change in the near future except perhaps in input peripheral equipment. However, this consideration apart, assuming the availability of resources to purchase a machine outright, comparative costs should be obtained of the annual hire cost including maintenance, and the annual capital cost of buying outright assessed over the useful life of the machine plus, again, the cost of maintenance. Other points to bear in mind if hiring are (a) the minimum length of time the manufacturer will contract for and (b) any restriction on the number of hours the machine may be operated in a week. Additional charges may be incurred for using the machine for more than the number of hours stipulated in the agreement.

THE COMPUTER PROJECT

The following are the main steps management must take to introduce computer methods.

1. Establish firm objectives. Motives for introducing a computer need to be examined, the uses to which it is to be put decided upon and an estimate made of the date at which the installation will become operational.

2. Make a preliminary study, including (a) investigation into alternative ways of achieving the same objectives (b) the education of the director made responsible for computer services, (c) getting as much information as possible on the problems likely to arise in transferring to computer operation the areas of work decided upon.

3. Conduct research into the consequences. Analyse the effect on the actual work that will be taken on. What benefits will arise? What changes in organisation will have to be made? What will be the effect on staff—redundancy, re-training, shift in responsibilities.

4. Make plans for introducing the changes. Draw up a time-table for implementing the changes. Allow reasonable time for staff re-training and attitudes to become accustomed to the idea of a computer. Plan communications and decide which members of staff are to be consulted. Plan staff movements and staff training.

5. Put the plan into action. Where possible do this in phases, reviewing each completed phase before moving on to the next. Leave room for flexibility to cover any unforeseen circumstances that may arise.

MANAGEMENT PROBLEMS

We now move to a review of some of the problems faced by management in putting computer systems into operation. Introducing a computer means change: changes in organisation, in areas of responsibility, in work load, in work flow, in work descipline and in physical environment. Change is not only unsettling while it lasts but it may also, in the long term, produce conditions that are unsatisfactory or unacceptable to some people. Management problems, by and large, centre around attitudes to, and the results of, the change brought about by the adoption of computer methods.

ATTITUDES TO CHANGE

As was mentioned above, change is unsettling both from an organisational and from an individual point of view. Attitudes to change are determined by a number of factors and vary very much from person to person. Some members of staff may well welcome change while others view it with grave misgivings. While it is hardly the province of this book to go deeply into the psycsology of change, some of the factors affecting peoples attitudes are worth mentioning. Age is significant, younger people generally accepting change more readily then older. Social responsibilities, upkeep of a home, care of children etc., may lead to an over-riding desire for security. A person's standing in the organisation, the prospects opened up by change and the rewards offered, and his individual personality will directly affect his attitude. Some of these factors are, of course, outside the control of the management but, nevertheless, management will want to implement changes as smoothly as possible and, as far as they can, to engender in their staff a favorable and enthusiastic attitude to the proposed changes. Factors within an organisation that will have an influence on staff attitudes are:

(*a*) *Past policy to change.*
Has the management dealt fairly and reasonably with members of staff involved in change in the past?

(*b*) *Relationships within the firm*
Are management-staff relationships such as to produce an atmosphere of confidence and co-operation, or, on the other hand, are staff suspicious of management motives?

(*c*) *Communications*
Knowledge that change is to happen without knowing the effects it will have on individuals gives rise to a great deal of speculation and rumour. A computer having been decided upon, while it may not be possible at this early stage to define the role each member of staff will play in relation to it, they must be kept informed of general aims and policy. However, a general statement of what is happening and why, is of less importance than being told 'what will happen to me?' Wherever possible, staff must be reassured about their continued security and standing within the organisation. Unless they know where they stand, key personnel will be tempted to 'play it safe' by getting a job elsewhere.

(*d*) *Participation and Identification*
In planning the detail of the change-over, existing staff should be involved as much as possible. This has both a practical aspect, as the people doing the job often know best what is going on, and the purpose of identifying them with the planning process.

(*e*) *Rewards*

Of course, a rational reaction to change is 'What am I going to get out of it'? Change will probably be welcomed if the end product is a more interesting or comfortable job, or greater financial reward. Planning policy must take into account that incentives may need to be offered.

(*f*) *Timing*

If any change is unsettling, hurried and unplanned change is very much more so, and repeatedly postponed changes only add to the confusion. Allow time in planning to ensure that all the requirements of the change can be met, and having set a date, keep to it.

Generally, then, management at director level must realise that the introduction of a computer will mean change. This change may not be welcomed by some staff and so management has a responsibility to encourage the acceptance of change and to plan its implementation with the minimum amount of upheaval.

THE COMPUTER AND MIDDLE MANAGEMENT

It is not unusual for the impact of the change-over to be felt most at middle management level, particularly by heads of departments. This problem needs special attention by management. The general effect of computer processing in relation to departmental structure is that some departments are completely eliminated, the staffing of others may be considerably reduced and departmental divisions tend to break down. In addition to this, since routine decision making will now largely be the province of the computer, the responsibilities of middle managers in this field are very much reduced.

Departments that are mainly concerned with routine processing will tend to disappear altogether. For example, an invoicing department that, having received advice notes from the stores, prices them, extends, deducts discounts and types a sales invoice for dispatch to the customer, need no longer exist when this processing is carried out electronically. In other departments, some functions may still be performed manually, while the bulk of the work is processed by computer. In a Wages Office, for example, the bulk of the work is concerned with the routine calculation of wages and the preparation of a pay-roll, all of which can be coped with by the computer, but a small amount of the work may be retained as manual procedures—individual tax statements for employees leaving, tax and pension returns to Inland Revenue etc. However, does the retention of this small amount of manual work justify the continued existence of a separate wages office?

In manual systems, work flow tends to progress from department to department. For example, details of a credit sale are recorded in the stores on an advice note, the advice note passes to the stock control department to record the issue, then to an invoicing department to price, extend and raise an invoice. Copies of the invoice then go to the Sales Department for Sales Analysis and to Accounts department for ledger posting. In a computer system, the one record prepared from the source document, in this case the advice note, will be used within the one department, the computer department, to prepare the invoice, up-date the stock records, up-date the sales ledger and provide the statistical information. This eliminates to a great extent the need for separate departments each processing the separate jobs within the one main business function—sales.

This all leads to the complete elimination of some departments and a tendency to merge the manual processing left in other departments on a more functional basis. The number of management posts at departmental level is reduced, and responsibilities are changed.

Another major effect on middle management centres around the ability of the computer to make routine decisions. Notoriously, a great deal of the department manager's time is taken up in sorting out problems arising from routine work. These decisions are often necessarily subjective, sometimes based on experience and know-how but without the detailed information necessary to reach an objective decision, or sometimes because too many variables are involved for adequate consideration. The human mind finds difficulty in making a decision if faced with more than two variables. The computer suffers from neither of these disadvantages. It can have all the information available at very short notice that is necessary to reach a decision, and it can take into account any number of variables. If correctly programmed the computer will not only make routine decisions far more quickly but also far more objectively. Not only are the routine decisions of the middle manager reduced, but also his role in making major policy decisions is diminished. Top management rely on middle management for the information on which they base policy decisions. With a computer in operation this reliance is to a great extent eliminated, the information being supplied direct from the computer department. Not only this, the computer eliminates to a great extent the time lag experienced with manual systems as information is gradually passed up through a chain of command. For example, if control totals are produced by a number of ledger clerks, summarised by the accounts office manager, edited by the accountant and then passed on to the financial director, even assuming each person in the chain does his work quickly (a large assumption) the results may well arrive at the top too late for quick corrective action to be taken. The computerised reduction of the time lag between performance and reporting, enables management to reach policy decisions in time for them to be effective. As a by-product of this, some policy decisions previously left to lower levels of management because of the time element and the information requirements, can now come within the province of top level management.

To summarise then, one important effect of a computer is, at high management level, to widen the area of decision making and to ensure that the information required to support policy decisions is available in time for them to be effective. At middle management level, it eliminates to a great extent the need for routine decision making and also eliminates the preparation of control information to support policy decisions made at top management level. Looked at from another point of view, however, one important advantage for middle management is that more time is available for supervising the work under their control and for planning and for developing new ideas.

STAFF

We have seen that the re-organisation inherent in the introduction of a computer will eventually lead to the displacement of staff. Experience shows that large scale redundancy is unlikely to result from the new processing methods. This is due largely to the fact that most of the routine manual processing is done by unskilled labour in which there is usually a fairly high labour turnover rate. Thus the problem of redundancy at this level has a tendency to solve itself. The problem of more highly skilled and therefore more permanent labour, however, has to be faced. Within a computer department a number of new posts will arise, of Systems Analysts, Programmers, Control staff, computer operators and so on. Most firms make a practice of recruiting much of this staff from within their own organisation and providing the necessary facilities for training. While it may be argued that it is better to recruit skilled programmers and analysts from outside, existing staff have the advantage of an intimate knowledge of the organisation and the policy and practices of their own firm, and they are known quantities as far as the management is concerned. In practice, the best policy is often a compromise between the two by appointing from outside the senior systems man and chief programmer, and recruiting the rest of the computer department staff from existing employees. Recruitment of staff for data preparation, that is, operators for punched cards, punched paper tape machines etc., usually presents no initial difficulty. Most firms employ operators for one kind of machine or another in connection with manual systems, and usually the operators displaced by the introduction of computer methods are prepared to be re-trained.

By and large then, staff redundancy is not usually a major problem. Normal wastage in the turnover of unskilled labour and the re-training and absorption of more senior members of staff in the new computer set-up obviates the need for management to dispense with the services of members of staff.

COMPUTER DEPARTMENT STAFF

There are two problems that management should be aware of as far as the staff of the computer department itself is concerned. The first is that the shortage of skilled computer staff. This, while being very evident at the moment, will probably be cured in time. There is still a fair amount of competition between computer users for trained staff which means that fairly high salaries must be paid to attract and keep the computer manager, systems, programming and operating staff. There is also a tendency for staff to be attracted by the capability of the machine. A firm with a new powerful machine can often attract staff more easily than a firm operating an older and less versatile machine.

We have already seen that one effect of a computer is to reduce the power and responsibilities of middle management, but the reverse side of the coin to this is that in doing so a great deal of power is placed in the hands of the small group of specialists staffing the computer department. The whole organisation can well become completely dependent on the computer staff for its routine processing needs and the management dependent for the control information required to make decisions. Perhaps one can go even further than this and say that even a small section of the department, for example the data preparation section, has the power to bring the whole processing and therefore the operation of the firm to a stand-still.

ENVIRONMENT

The physical conditions demanded by the computer itself—temperature, humidity, air filtration etc.—will be stipulated by the manufacturer concerned. Perhaps it would be as well to mention in this section on management problems more specifically those parts of an installation concerned with data preparation. The preparation of punched cards or punched paper tape tends to be repetitive, uninteresting and boring but the whole processing service depends on the accuracy and punctuality with which this work is performed. Working conditions should be such as to promote efficient preparation of data. Apart from a pleasant physical environment, work loads and work flow should be organised so as to get the best out of the operators. In particular, the more exacting punching jobs should be fairly distributed, and should be kept reasonably small so that punch operators are presented with jobs whose end is quickly attainable rather than ones seeming to be endless.

INCREASED WORK LOAD DURING IMPLEMENTATION

Another problem faced by management is the very heavy work load during the change-over period, occasioned by the transfer of manual records to computer files and the probably need to run both manual and computer systems for a time in order to check the latter. Unless plans are formulated well in advance to cope with this extra work, take-on dates could well be delayed. A sufficiently interested staff, will often be prepared to help by working overtime although the temporary transfer of staff from other less vital activities or the employment of temporary staff are other ways of dealing with the problem.

MACHINE FAILURE

Modern computers regularly and efficiently maintained and in the hands of adequately trained operators, are very reliable pieces of equipment. However, even in the best run installations the possibility of a lengthy breakdown cannot be ignored. To insure against this, most firms enter into a reciprocal 'stand-by' agreement with another firm operating a similar machine. This ensures that with the machine out of action vital jobs can still be processed.

COSTS

While it is impractical to quote prices of individual computers, either purchased outright or rented, the following is an attempt to set down the main items of cost other than the computer itself, when setting up a computer department. It should be emphasised, however, that it is much more difficult to accurately assess the costs incurred, and indeed the benefits derived, than for most other forms of capital investment.

Costs can be classified under the main headings of accommodation, hardware, investigation and development, and maintenance.

(a) Accommodation

Basic requirements are a computer room, data preparation section, accommodation for file and paper storage, offices for Systems Analysts and Programmers, Control room and reception centre, Computer Manager's office and work-room for maintenance engineers. Over and above this provision will probably have to be made for air-conditioning equipment for at least the computer room and library.

In practice it is found that the space required by a computer installation is less than that needed to accommodate the personnel, machines and materials used for manual systems for an equivalent work load. Also, whereas in manual systems, accommodation requirements tend to increase in proportion to increase in work volumes, a computer is able to considerably increase its turnover of work with only need, perhaps, for extra space for the additional machines to cope with data preparation.

(b) Hardware

Hardware, of course, is the major cost element, and usually these requirements are assessed at the feasibility study stage. However, it is as well to bear in mind from the outset that detailed systems investigation may indicate a need for more equipment than that considered necessary at the feasibility study. For example, it may be found that additional backing storage is required. Hardware costs fall into four main groups (I) The computer itself. That is the Central Processor, and Peripheral equipment which would normally consist of input and output devices, and backing storage. (II) Data Preparation equipment, Punching and Verifying machines and possibly card tabulator's and sorters. (III) Ancillary equipment for output handling, guillotines, bursters, collators, folding machines etc., and (IV) the provision of storage equipment, racks, cupboards, safes for high security documents, desks etc.

(c) Investigation and development costs

This is the most difficult cost item to estimate. As far as the feasibility study is concerned, if the manufacturer takes this on, on the basis of obtaining the order for the machine, then there will be probably no charge. A firm proposing to spend £100,000—£200,000 on equipment, rather than relying on one manufacturer, would probably prefer a completely independent investigation by a consultant. For a full scale investigation a fee of £10,000 or more could well be incurred. An alternative approach, to cut costs at this initial stage, is for the prospective user to appoint a team of say three people from his own staff, possibly from an existing Organisation and Methods department, to carry out the investigation, and call in consultants to check through and advise on the report they prepare.

As far as systems development and programming costs are concerned, while the number of analysts and programmers to be employed can be fixed fairly accurately, the time they will take to bring systems to an operational point is very difficult to estimate. A number of variables are involved. The experience and know-how of the staff, unforeseen complications in design, the degree of turn-over within the systems and programming teams. As a generalisation it must be said that this cost had a tendency to escalate, resulting in performance costs being well in excess of estimates. This can be mitigated to a certain extent by making sure that at least one team member has previous practical experience in developing similar systems.

(d) Operating costs

Once the system has settled down and become fully operational, discounting rental charges for the machine should this be appropriate, the main cost elements are, of course, accommodation, staff, supplies and machine maintenance. Systems having been imple-mented, the requirements for systems and programming staff will very much decrease. The need for systems maintenance, however, still exists although the systems and programming staff required for this purpose is probably only in the region of 20 per cent of that required during development.

It is not easy to assess objectively savings that arise through using a computer. As has been pointed out, the argument that computers result in staff savings is not usually borne out by experience, except, perhaps when very high volumes of routine processing are taken over from unskilled clerical labour. But even then it must be kept in mind that the cost of trained computer staff can be individually two or three times as high as the unskilled labour they replace. Other direct savings may be in the cost of equipment no longer needed—accounting, calculating machines etc. —and in savings in accommodation.

Generally speaking, cost benefits tend to be of an indirect character. For example, a computer Sales Ledger system will probably get customer sales statements out earlier, thus encouraging earlier payment and so improving cash availability. A computer stock inventory system may lead to lower stock levels being maintained resulting in savings in storage costs and releasing cash otherwise tied up in sticks. This type of saving however is difficult to measure in advance.

EXERCISES CHAPTER 14

1. It has been suggested by members of your firm that a digital computer would be a valuable asset.
   Briefly suggest the constitution of a committee that you would set up to examine the project.
   What points would you look for before agreeing to the installation?
   (Royal Society of Arts—Computer Appreciation—Stage II)

2. Why do you think it desirable that management at director level should be actively involved in implementing a computer project?

3. What are the probable effects on management at departmental level of the introduction of computer systems?

4. What main advantages would you expect to accrue from the introduction of a computer installation to carry out routine clerical procedures?

5. What main items of cost would you expect to be incurred in the introduction of a computer department for processing commercial systems?

6. List some of the circumstances that you feel might give rise to management initially thinking in terms of a changeover to computer methods.

7. As a manager responsible for implementing computer systems, what actions would you take to minimise the disruption caused by the changeover.

8. What are the main steps involved in planning the installation of a computer.

9. 'Since one role of a computer is to make routine decisions, this obviates the need for middle management'. Discuss this statement.

10. 'The introduction of a computer tends towards the breakdown of departmental barriers'. Explain why this is so.

11. What investigations should a company make before a decision is made whether or not to purchase a computer for its commercial work?
    (Institute of Data Processing)

Index

All references are to page numbers.
Numbers in **bold type** indicate a diagram or illustration.
Where several page numbers are given for one topic, the most important reference is printed in *italics*.

Example:

Flowcharts, *109–124*, 159, 160, **199–201** means that although flowcharts are mentioned on pages 159 and 160, the main discussion is on pages 109 to 124, and there are illustrations on pages 199 to 201.